By The Editors of Consumer Guide®

Kitchen Remodeling Made Easy

Contents

Printed and bound by Graficki Zavod Hrvatske & Printing House
Founded 1874

2 3 4 5 6 7 8 9 10

Library of Congress Catalog Card Number: 80-81970

Publications International, Ltd. has made every effort to ensure accuracy and reliability of the information, instructions and directions in this book; however, it is in no way to be construed as a guarantee, and Publications International, Ltd. is not liable in case of misinterpretations of the directions, human error or typographical mistakes.

Introduction

Take two small rooms, kitchen and dining space, and combine them into one spacious, breathtaking area of your home. Large windows and ceiling beams enhance aura of luxury created by huge food preparation/eating facilities.

Transforming a kitchen from old to new is not a simple task. The key to success lies in step-by-step planning, rather than trial and error. Even if you only have the time and budget for changing one feature, that change can be part of a larger plan.

Perhaps you just want to replace appliances in an older home. That would update your kitchen, but you would not be remodeling it. If you really want a kitchen that suits your lifestyle, a kitchen that fits your patterns of socializing, of entertaining, of meeting the needs and tastes of your family, then replacing appliances is not enough.

So the first step is *not* to rush out and buy new appliances to replace the old ones. The first step is to sit down with other members of the household and ask questions. The answers you write down will outline your needs. Once you know your needs, you can evaluate how well your present kitchen meets them. If a sizable discrepancy exists between your needs and your present kitchen's ability to meet those needs, you know that the time has come to consider remodeling your kitchen.

ASSESSING YOUR PRESENT KITCHEN

The numbers after each question indicate how satisfactory you find the various elements of your kitchen. Circle the number indicating your degree of satisfaction, from number 1 for very poor to number 6 for very good. Then tally up the total of all circled numbers and check the scale below.

Poor 1 2 3 4 5 6 Good

Storage space. Is there enough storage space and is it easily accessible? Do you need a stepladder or stool to reach shelves? Do you often have to walk across the room for items not stored in the right place? *1 2 3 4 5 6*

Work space. Is there enough counter space for preparing food and for cleanup chores?
1 2 3 4 5 6

Up-to-date appliances. How many more years can you count on your present appliances? If new ones are in the budget and schedule, be sure to find the most energy-efficient appliances, otherwise operation cost may exceed the original price. Are you considering adding appliances, like a microwave oven or trash compactor?
1 2 3 4 5 6

Ventilation. Does your range have a hood vented to the outside? If you have a separate wall oven, is it vented to the outside? Is venting power-ful enough to prevent grease deposits on walls and cabinets? *1 2 3 4 5 6*

Lighting. Do you have both general illumination and task lighting on counters? Can you see easily into drawers? Can you work without being in your own shadow? *1 2 3 4 5 6*

Efficiency. Is the work triangle efficient? By work triangle, we mean the distance between the sink, refrigerator and range—the three main features of the kitchen. Many kitchen designers recommend that the total distance from the front center of your sink to your refrigerator then to your cooktop be at least 12 feet but not more than 22 feet. *1 2 3 4 5 6*

Nuisances. Does the oven door or the refrigerator door open across the entry door so that traffic is blocked? Does the refrigerator door open away from the action instead of toward it?
1 2 3 4 5 6

Subjective factors. Are you satisfied with the color in your kitchen? Is the kitchen large enough? Too large? Is the general look dingy or depressing? Is it closed off from the rest of the house? Do you like the cabinet style? Do you have the modern features you would like?
1 2 3 4 5 6

Your Kitchen Score—Add and Total Here _____

8-16: You are working under a severe handicap. Your kitchen is seriously inadequate.

17-24 Your kitchen has many shortcomings that could be improved.

25-32: Although you're not in bad shape, you still would benefit from a remodeling of your kitchen.

33-40: Your problems are rather specific. *Kitchen Remodeling Made Easy* can help you isolate and correct them.

41-48: You are the exception. Give this book to someone who needs it.

EVALUATING YOUR KITCHEN NEEDS

Nobody, neither you nor a skilled kitchen designer, can design your kitchen properly without knowing the answers to many questions.

Regular stock kitchen cabinets can create an attractive wet bar. Abundant storage capacity is an additional benefit.

Here are some of the questions specialists would ask you. The answers should form the basis for planning and designing your new kitchen.

How big is your household? Size of the family relates directly to the amount of storage space you need in cabinets for dishes and foods. Identifying family members, with ages, can help in several ways. If there are young children in the family, you may want an "open" kitchen so you can keep an eye on them in adjacent rooms. Teenage children leaving soon for college or elsewhere make some storage needs only temporary.

Do you like to cook? If you really like to cook you may need a more versatile range, more counter space for food preparation, a larger refrigerator, and more storage for utensils and cookware. If there is more than one chef in the family, a peninsula, island or extra food-preparation center might be in order.

Do you like to entertain? If so, you might consider a wet bar, a wine rack, storage for more glassware and other dishes, a punch bowl, etc. Storage problems can be considerable.

What are your shopping habits? Some families do heavy grocery shopping weekly or biweekly. They might need a separate freezer or a big pantry cabinet.

Are you super-fastidious? Do you like everything off the counters and behind doors? Or are you the more casual, open-shelf type who enjoys an array of collectibles in the kitchen. One person's clutter is another's antique collection. Also, some people do not mind spending time taking care of items like ceramic cooktops that need daily attention. The amount of care required by some kitchen material is considerable, and you should know before you buy.

What is the motif of your other home furnishings? A kitchen should compliment the other rooms in the home. Other furnishings can supply the key to color preferences, use of fabrics, wall coverings, etc. Ask the rest of the family if they really like what they have.

Do husband and wife both work? A working couple often wants to minimize the time spent in the kitchen. Efficient design is most important. Appliances like microwave ovens, a dishwasher, a disposer, and a compactor may be time-savers, too.

How careful are household members? Safety can be built into a kitchen. Household cleaners usually go in the under-sink cabinet, but storage might have to be placed higher or in a locked pantry if small children are around. Range controls and ceramic cooktops can be hazardous to children and should be made inaccessible to small hands.

What are your family seating habits and preferences? This determines how much dining space is needed in the kitchen. Do you want eating space just for the children or for the whole family, part of a peninsula or island, or a formal area for separate table and chairs?

BUDGET

After you have assessed your present kitchen and evaluated your needs, there is one more very important consideration—budget. Your needs may be vast and your budget only able to cover cosmetic changes like wallpaper and paint. Full-scale remodeling is a major investment, as well as a time-consuming project.

If you are going to stay in the house for an in-definite time and have no intention of selling or moving, it may make more sense to go all the way with a major remodeling job than if you plan to move soon.

If you are planning the kitchen improvement to increase the resale value of the house, then you want to make the kitchen look as great as possible without spending too much money on it. Just about any improvement in the kitchen can be considered an investment that will pay off in increasing resale value, but if your house is valued at $60,000 in a neighborhood of $60,000 homes, a $10,000 kitchen will not increase its value to $70,000. In such a case, it is better to spend $2,000 or $3,000 on the kitchen to build your house value up to $65,000. And it can do that.

With these considerations in mind, let's make a quick survey of some of the choices you have.

COSMETIC ALTERATIONS

Alterations that are done purely for aesthetic reasons are not different, basically, from changing hair color or selecting and applying nail polish and lipstick. They are not basic changes. They are changes in appearance.

Wall Treatments

Chances are the walls you have are painted. They can be repainted in new, different colors. You can add painted graphics, available in most areas at home centers, art, stationery or variety stores. But for kitchen use, be sure you select a high-quality paint that is easy to clean.

Ceramic tile is a beautiful and excellent material for the backsplash area—the part of the wall between the counter and the wall cabinets.

Wood paneling or wood planks are popular materials for one or more walls in the kitchen, to add variety in color and texture.

Vertical-grade plastic laminates—thinner grades of the material found on most of the nation's countertops—are good as wall material. They are extremely easy to clean, can be bought at most home centers in a tremendous variety of colors and patterns, and are good for backsplash or other wall areas. However, they should not be applied on the wall behind the cooktop because the heat will tend to discolor them. Corian, made by the DuPont Company, another countertop material, is also available as a wall covering. It simulates marble.

Vinyl-surfaced wall fabrics are one of the most popular materials for kitchen walls. The range of colors and patterns is practically limitless, and they are easy to apply and maintain.

Stumped for a place to put a home office? Foldaway desk and chair (with nearby cabinets) create a useful mini-office in the kitchen.

Fabrics can be used on walls away from cooking areas with very decorative effects. Sometimes they are used for accent walls, but often a decorator will use pre-glued fabric to match draperies and surface an entire wall or ceiling with them.

Brick and stone in their natural forms can pose cleaning and weight problems. There are, however, plastic-based simulations of these materials that are light, easy to apply, realistic in appearance, and more easily cleaned. These could be overpowering if too much were used, but they can be very good for an accent wall.

Kitchen carpeting can be used on walls, coved from the floor all the way to the ceiling or, more often, up to wainscot height, capped by a strip of molding. Kitchen carpeting has a sponge rubber backing, separated from the surface by a waterproof membrane that makes it easy to wash. It is light in weight and easy to apply.

Ceiling Treatments

The standard treatment is paint, usually in a light color because darker colors tend to "lower" a ceiling in a room that often is small.

One of the best alternatives to paint is acoustical tile. This can be applied directly to the old ceiling, but it is especially useful when the ceiling is high (more than 96 inches) and when it is used in a suspended ceiling system. Ideally, this suspended ceiling system will incorporate fluorescent lighting panels designed for the system. It helps muffle the many noises of the kitchen (disposer, dishwasher, blender, etc.) and is easy to put up, although it takes care.

Wall coverings often are used on the ceiling. They should be fabric-backed and vinyl-surfaced.

Ceiling beams are a popular accessory treatment for a kitchen. Beams can be bought ready-made, either of solid wood or hollow, or they are relatively easy to make with ¼-inch plywood. Easiest, probably, is to buy prefinished plastic beams. Not only are they fairly realistic, but they are so light that they can be applied easily with adhesive.

Floor Treatments

Your choice for floors include the various resilient materials in combinations of vinyl and asbestos or vinyl alone, in sheets or easy-to-lay squares, cushioned or uncushioned; wood, in finished planks or parquet; carpeting; or ceramic tile.

The standard of past years, linoleum, is no longer made in this country. It has been replaced by the more modern vinyl and vinyl/asbestos materials.

Sheet goods generally cost more and present more of an installation problem. The adhesive-backed place-and-press tiles are easiest to install.

Countertops

Countertops can be very decorative, so a change in the countertops should be considered as one of the possible cosmetic alternatives.

The decorative laminates on countertops provided by builders usually have somewhat muted patterns, appearing slightly greenish or yellowish from a distance of a few feet. Supposedly, these colors go with any appliance or cabinet. But you,

Limited kitchen storage capacity can be increased by adding a custom cooktop island. Island shelving, cabinet dividers, etc., are carefully matched to specific storage needs. Overhead vent hood and light enhance utility of cooktop area.

in your own kitchen, know specifically what appliances and cabinets you have, so you can be bolder in selecting from the hundreds of colors, patterns and woodgrain available. Countertop inserts, such as tile squares or a wooden butcher block, can improve appearance immensely.

Cabinet Refacing

Whether your kitchen cabinets are wood, plastic-laminated or steel, you can change their looks without actually replacing them.

If they are painted and the old paint is smooth,

you can simply repaint them, after minor sanding, using a gloss enamel. Or, you can remove the old finish and apply new stain and lacquer, antiquing if you wish.

If the cabinets are plastic laminate in a dark woodgrain pattern, and if the laminate is in good condition, you can buy new laminate and apply it over the old, using the lighter woodgrains that are more fashionable today, a butcher block pattern or a solid color. Or, you can send the doors and drawer fronts to a plastic fabricator and have the job done professionally. Then you could paint the exposed face frame and end panels in a matching or somewhat darker color for a new look.

The older, steel cabinets that were so prevalent in the 1950's can be painted or covered with sheets of plastic laminate. You can buy sheets of laminate and cut them to size.

Another way, especially if the old doors are battered, is to buy new doors and drawer fronts to replace the old. Nearly all cabinets, except those built on-site by carpenters, are built in modular widths and in standard heights. So companies now specialize in making replacement doors and drawer fronts. Many of these are wood, and many are made of polyurethane and finished to look like wood.

FUNCTIONAL ALTERNATIVES

While cosmetic changes make your kitchen look better, functional changes make it work better. Here we are talking about things you can do short of remodeling, keeping the basic layout. You might need to replace the appliances. You almost surely need new lighting—most kitchens do. Sometimes a simple rearrangement of elements is effective. And sometimes it is possible to add a simple island or peninsula for more storage or work space, or to shorten the work triangle.

Sink Replacement

The sink might be part of your replacement project. Sinks get a lot of use and deteriorate with age. Or you might want to replace a single-bowl model with a double-bowl or triple-bowl. Equally important, you might want to replace old, worn faucets with a handsome new single-lever faucet-and-spout assembly, and you might want soap and lotion dispensers or an instant hot water attachment. Another worthwhile option is installation of water purification equipment in the sink cabinet. Many faucets have flow restrictors that automatically can cut water use by as much as 50 percent.

Pressed-steel, porcelain-enameled sinks are the lowest-priced. High-quality stainless sinks are the most expensive. Cast-iron sinks now come in a wide range of bright colors as well as white. Another alternative is a Corian sink, a man-made marble, which is formed as an integral part of a Corian material countertop. This is quite expensive.

Lighting

When you find yourself working in your own shadow, when you find it difficult to read recipes or to see into kitchen drawers, you have a lighting problem. A poorly lighted kitchen is worse than an inconvenient kitchen; it is an unsafe kitchen. You need three kinds of lighting in your kitchen:

• General lighting, for overall illumination, creates a pleasant environment and lets you see into cabinets and opened drawers.

• Task lighting beams more intense light directly on jobs at the range and sink, and the countertop work surfaces.

• Decorative lighting is for special purposes, such as separating a dining nook or eating peninsula from the rest of the kitchen, or to accent a decorative wall.

The two artificial light sources you can choose are incandescent or fluorescent fixtures. Incandescence provides a warmer light and is better if your kitchen colors are in the red-yellow-brown tones. Fluorescent lighting casts a cold light that favors blues and greens; it tends to flatten out the rich appearance of wood cabinets.

Natural daylight, of course, is a third source, and it can come from windows or from a skylight; but it doesn't lessen the need for other lights.

REMODELING

The average full-scale remodeling job in a kitchen today, with replacement of cabinets and appliances and a changed layout, is more than $6,000. On a do-it-yourself basis, you might cut up to 30 percent off that.

Why remodel, when it is so expensive? One reason is that your kitchen is wasteful or unsuitable for your needs. Another reason is that you want to, either because you are tired of the old kitchen, or you want to increase the value of the house for resale.

When should you remodel? When there is a change in your lifestyle, because of marriage, divorce, additions to the family, loss of family members, new social habits, increase in income, and because if you delay it will only become more expensive.

Creative positioning of cooktop/work area around wall projection maximizes usable space. Snack bar set in open wall augments storage capacity while providing eat-in facilities in the kitchen.

You can cut the price, of course, by choosing to remodel only partially. A combination of cosmetic and functional changes can amount to a partial remodeling, but that kind of updating and replacing may fall short of creating a kitchen that's uniquely yours and yours alone.

Partial remodeling can be the first step in a long-range remodeling plan. A long-range plan would call for a total redesign job on your present kitchen, with floor plan and elevation drawings showing its entirety. You could figure out a timetable for step-by-step completion over a period of a year or two. This stretches out the payments. First you change the elements most needed. Then each new element gradually would complete the new design.

Partial remodeling might include rearranging appliances, adding new countertops, replacing appliances or adding a peninsula or island. With a peninsula or island you may gain a new location for a sink or range. Or you may gain needed work space or eating area.

Plan And Design Your Own Kitchen

Designing a kitchen is a game of inches. Since you will be buying and installing a number of cabinets and appliances—all of which have specific sizes—there is no room for error. So one of the first steps in planning and designing a kitchen is to measure the available space accurately and to record your measurements on paper.

For accuracy, use a 6-foot folding carpenter's rule when measuring. A household yardstick is much too short, and a retractable steel tape measure can sag or slip.

Measure all room dimensions to within 1/16 inch, and record each measurement as accurately as possible. Remember, even a very slight error can mean significant difficulties later. For example, if the space you think can accommodate 120 inches of cabinets and appliances turns out to be no more than 119½ inches, your original plan may prove unfeasible.

Before you start taking measurements, make a rough outline of the entire room on a grid sheet where each square, for example, is equal to 3 inches. Then begin at one corner and measure the distance from the corner to a window's trim at a height of 36 inches above the floor (the height of a countertop). Proceed by measuring from the outside of the window trim on one side of the window trim to the outside of the trim on the other side, from that trim edge to the door trim, and so on, recording each measurement accurately on your grid sheet. Write each measurement down as you go along without trying to add them up. Adding them as you go along diverts your attention and can lead to error. Be sure to note all obstacles—chimney, offsets, radiators, etc.—on the grid sheet. Also indicate the locations of all existing electrical outlets, light switches, and fixtures.

As you finish measuring a wall, total all the figures. Then make another overall measurement to check your addition. If you discover any discrepancy, start all over again.

Now indicate on the sketch where all doors lead, door and windowsill heights, and the height from the windowsill to the top of window trim. Also measure and indicate the height of the ceilings, from floor to ceiling, and the height and depth of the existing soffit (the wall area above the upper cabinets); soffit height should be measured from the floor to the soffit.

Mark the locations for the sink drain and the incoming water supply on the grid sheet, but keep in mind that you can move the sink somewhat to one side or the other; all you have to do is turn and extend the drain trap (it need not go straight into the wall) and extend the supply lines to the faucets.

It is essential that you check the squareness of the room's corners because they are seldom perfectly square. Such discrepancies must be considered. To check the corners, mark a point precisely 36 inches out from the corner along one wall at a height of 36 inches above the floor. Do the same for the other corner wall, but at a distance of 48 inches from the corner. Now measure the direct distance between the two points (the hypotenuse of what is supposed to be a right triangle). This distance should be exactly 60 inches. If it is less, the angle between the two walls is less than 90 degrees; if it is more, the angle is more than 90 degrees. Make a note of any lack of squareness so that your countertop can be cut to match the actual shape of the corner.

Draw the entire room on your grid sheet, not just the walls that will be in your kitchen installation. The distances to other walls or parts of the room are important. And where you find corners out of square, be sure to note both the distance along the wall and the distance 24 inches out from the wall; you will have to plan your kitchen for the shorter measurement because the cabinets will not fit if sized for the longer measurement.

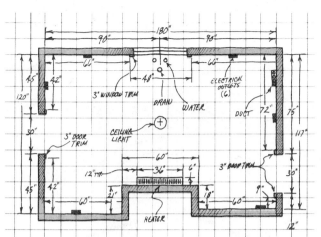

Before measuring, make a rough outline of the entire room on a grid sheet. Then measure all room dimensions to within 1/16th of an inch.

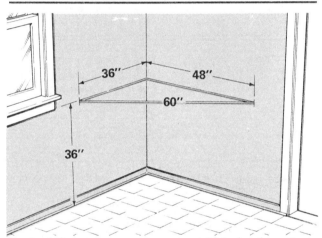

To check for squareness, measure out 36 inches from the corner along one wall and 48 inches out along the other. The distance between the two points (if the walls are square) should be exactly 60 inches.

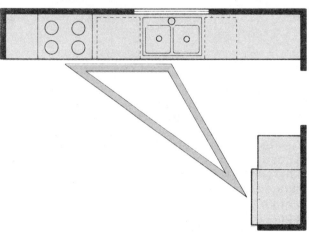

A door within an L-shaped kitchen allows traffic to cross the work triangle, creating a safety hazard.

With an accurate sketch of the room in front of you, you can proceed to design the kind of kitchen you want.

DESIGN SAFETY INTO THE KITCHEN

Many potentially hazardous activities take place in the kitchen. In addition to cutting, chopping, grinding, and slicing, people are often handling hot items, probing into drawers and cabinets, and operating electrical appliances.

This means that the kitchen is a place where accidents can happen. Although most accidents are attributable to human carelessness, the kitchen itself can be designed so as to make the probability of accidents far less likely and to reduce the severity of the accidents when they do occur.

The key to kitchen safety is to maximize efficiency and to minimize potential hazards. Here are some guidelines:

1. Make sure your kitchen offers an efficient and effective work triangle. This means that the total distance from sink to range to refrigerator should not be less than 12 feet nor more than 22 feet. Specifically, the various work areas should not be closer than 4 feet nor farther than 9 feet from one another. Less distance means you are too cramped, more means you must constantly take extra tiring steps.

2. Make sure your kitchen is well lighted, with sufficient general and "task" lighting.

3. Make sure your kitchen offers ample storage space and that access to the items stored poses no danger. Shelf space higher than 72 inches above the floor can present a hazard because a stool or ladder is usually required to reach things stored there.

4. Make sure you have ample counter space, including the proper amount of work space alongside the range and refrigerator. Otherwise, you will be doing too much transporting of hot pans and cold foods.

5. Minimize the number of sharp corners in your kitchen. Square corners on island or peninsula tops are hazardous to hips and hands, and should be rounded.

6. Vent hoods should be at least 56 inches above the floor and not protrude more than 18 inches from the wall. A hood that protrudes more than 18 inches should be moved slightly higher. If a vent hood needs to be more than 60 inches above the floor (for instance, if the cook is much taller than 6 feet), a more powerful vent fan will be needed to compensate for the loss in venting efficiency.

7. Avoid the exasperation of a refrigerator door that does not open into the work triangle; of oven or other appliance doors that block doorways or

This represents faulty planning. There should be at least 15 inches of counter space on the working side of the oven when oven and cooktop are separate units.

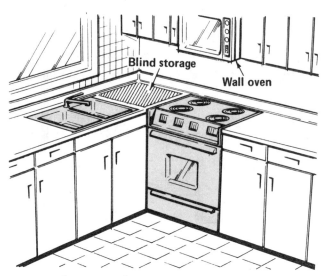

For safety's sake, don't position the range next to the sink. This situation also results in a loss of storage space in the corner.

Don't let room/refrigerator doors fight each other.

Don't make sink cabinet/dishwasher doors fight each other.

bump each other when opened; of appliances placed too close together or too close to either a wall or corner so that the action of doors or drawers is inhibited.

8. When selecting a new range and positioning it in the kitchen, consider the fire and burn hazard. You should not be forced to reach over steaming pots to reach the controls, and the burners should not be near window curtains and combustible wall coverings.

9. Garbage disposers must be handled with caution. Although batch-feed models usually require that a cover be put in place before operation can occur, insertion of a hand has been known to activate the batch-feed type. Continuous-feed disposers are activated by a switch. You can have a batch-feed disposer turned into a switch-operated unit for safety; if you do so, be sure to position the switch at least 6 feet from the disposer for maximum safety. Of course, the same distance between switch and disposer applies to continuous-feed units.

THE ACTIVITY CENTERS

Storage areas, countertop work space, and appliances form the activity centers of the kitchen: the sink, the range or cooktop, the refrigerator/freezer, the food preparation center, and the serving center.

The best place to start designing and planning your kitchen is usually the window. Since most homeowners want the sink under the window, that is where the plumbing lines generally are located. Thus, one element may be in place already. If you want to reserve the window for an eating area, you can move the plumbing lines, but doing so can get expensive and complicated. It should be avoided unless you are willing to add to your remodeling costs.

Assuming that the plumbing lines will stay where they are, consider storage space and counter work space. You must provide for enough of both, and you must position both in the right places.

The idea behind efficient storage is to store everything at the point of first use. For example, dinner dishes should be stored as close as possible to the dining area where they are first used. If this is impractical, they should be stored at the point of last use—near the dishwasher and sink.

When considering the things you must store, think about basic activity centers of the kitchen. The following list of items to be stored and the best locations for storing them should help you to plan a kitchen for maximum storage efficiency.

• Utensils. The tools of the kitchen include pots and pans, cutlery, baking dishes and so on. They are best stored near the range.

• Dinnerware. Store fine china in or near a separate dining room; store everyday dishes near the eat-in kitchen area.

• Food. Place packaged, canned, and bottled groceries (generally plan on a week's supply) in cabinets, ideally in a tall pantry cabinet with revolving or swing-out shelves. Fresh perishables go in a refrigerator freezer, except for potatoes, onions and the like, which should be stored in bins or drawers. All food storage areas should be as near as possible to the food preparation center.

• Cleaning supplies. Soaps, detergents, and cleaning implements generally go in an under-the-sink cabinet, while bigger items such as mops and brooms can be concealed in a tall utility cabinet; the utility cabinet need not be located in the kitchen as long as it is handy.

• Linens, paper goods, place mats, and other items. It is a good idea to get these items out of the way. A paper caddy with paper towels, alu-

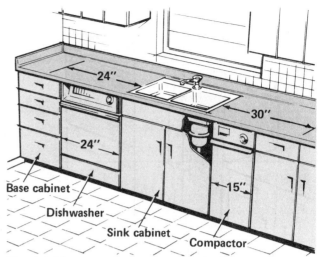

The sink/cleanup center recommended minimum counter space.

minum foil, and plastic wrap can be recessed into a wall near the food preparation or cleanup center. Linens should be placed in a drawer. All of these item, though, should be stored near the point of first use.

• Small appliances. As manufacturers produce more highly specialized appliances (to make a hamburger, to make a pizza, to pop corn, to broil, to open cans, to toast, to mix, etc.), storing these devices in the kitchen is often a big problem. A severe case of countertop clutter is common these days. One answer is to build in as many small appliances as you can. There are toasters and electric can openers that can be recessed into the wall. There are mixing centers with a base that is built into the countertop. Separate attachments for food processing, mixing, blending, meat grinding, knife sharpening, can opening, ice crushing, fruit squeezing and other functions can be stored in one cabinet beneath the counter, leaving nothing but a metal plate on the countertop.

• Trash. Although trash quickly exits the room, you must plan a temporary storage place for it. A trash compactor can be particularly valuable for a large family, especially if the unit can be built in where a cabinet would otherwise go. Most compactors take up the space of a 15-inch base cabinet, although at least one brand can fit in a 12-inch space.

The sink area includes a minimum of 30 inches of counter space to the right of the sink and 24 inches to the left (for right-handed persons), dishwasher adjacent (usually on the left), disposer under the sink, and compactor on the right. A double-bowl sink is very handy—even when the sink area includes a dishwasher—if

Refrigerator and wall oven each need separate counter space and therefore should not be placed next to each other.

space permits. This area should contain storage facilities for foods that need washing and for fruits and vegetables that do not go into the refrigerator. Cabinets with roll-out bins or shelves are ideal for such purposes. While most cooking pots and pans belong near the range, sauce pans and the coffeepot go best in the sink center.

The range or cooktop area should include at least 18 inches of counter space on either side; a ventilating hood and fan above; and storage for pots, pans, seasonings, and cooking utensils. If the cooktop and oven are separate, allow 15 inches of countertop space on the working side of the oven.

The refrigerator/freezer area should have a minimum counter work space of 18 inches on the door-opening side. The popular side-by-side refrigerator/freezers defeat this design principle because the refrigerator side is always on the right, and the freezer side on the left. Since the door-swing on such models is a short arc, however, the side-by-side unit seldom presents any serious interference problems. The refrigerator and freezer doors should open more than 90 degrees so that crispers and shelves can be easily removed. The refrigerator is the hub of the food storage center, so kitchen planners try to incorporate other food storage facilities—for example, base cabinets or a pantry cabinet—close by.

The food preparation center requires at least 36 inches of counter space, generally between the sink and range or between the sink and refrigerator.

The serving center is usually positioned near the cooking center; ideally, it should be between the cooking center and the eating area. It requires 30 inches of counter space for serving; and for storing trays, platters, serving dishes, napkins and the like.

Note that you can combine many counter space requirements. For example, the 30 inches needed to the right of the sink can be part of the 36 inches of space needed for a food preparation center.

PLANNING THE KITCHEN LAYOUT

Once the sink is placed, you know how to go about supplying the storage and counter needs for it. You know that the range goes to the left of the sink and that the refrigerator goes to its right. You also know the storage and counter needs of these two activity centers. Or do you?

Up to now we have been talking in averages and minimums. You, however, might need *more* countertop or *more* storage space. Remember, in your kitchen you have to make compromises between what you need, what you would like, and the space available. The way you resolve these opposing factors is what makes the kitchen uniquely yours.

You should always keep in mind, though, that you want to end up with a work triangle of not less than 12 feet and not more than 22 feet. The work triangle is, quite simply, the straight-line distance

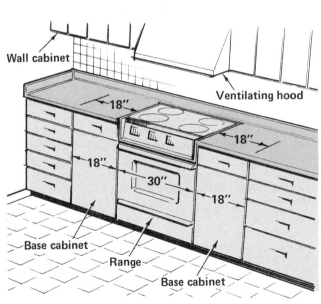

The cooking center recommended minimum counter space.

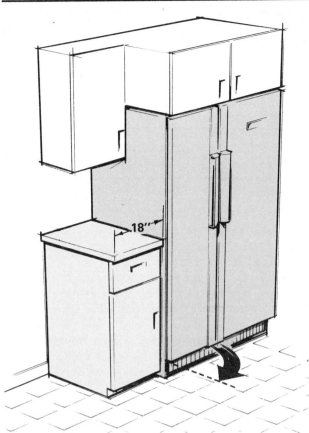

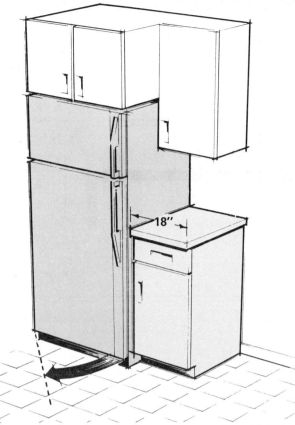

With a side-by-side unit, the work space can be on the left since the freezer door-swing makes a short arc.

The refrigerator/freezer area should have at least 18 inches of counter work space on the door-opening side.

between the center fronts of the sink and range, range and refrigerator, and refrigerator and sink. As we said, no two of the basic activity centers in a kitchen should be less than 4 feet apart nor greater than 9 feet apart. The following distances are considered ideal: sink to range—4 to 6 feet; range to refrigerator—4 to 9 feet; refrigerator to sink—4 to 7 feet. There are several kitchen layouts that will fulfill these requirements.

The one-wall kitchen is the simplest possible layout. Obviously, there will be no work triangle when the entire kitchen is along one wall. The one-wall layout can provide ample storage and work space, but in doing so it usually puts too much distance between the work centers on the flanks. A single person or a couple might be able to tolerate a one-wall kitchen. But generally, it is not an efficient kitchen, and almost never is it a desirable one.

The corridor kitchen that is open on both ends, permitting traffic to cross two legs of the work triangle, is another kitchen layout to be avoided. A closed corridor, on the other hand, can be very efficient. Often called a "Pullman" kitchen, the cor-

ridor has two work centers on one side, one on the other, and a minimum of 48 inches clearance in between. Since cabinets and appliances take up 2 feet on either wall, a corridor layout requires a kitchen that is at least 8 feet wide.

The L-shaped kitchen is quite common and makes for a very efficient work triangle that is open to other activities such as eating and recrea-

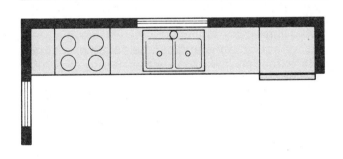

The one-wall kitchen is undesirable because it puts too much distance between the work centers on the flanks.

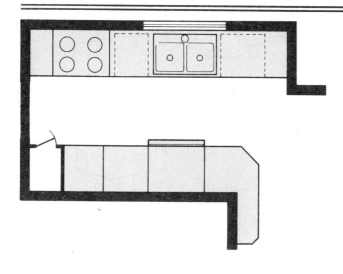

The corridor kitchen has two work centers on one wall and one on the other.

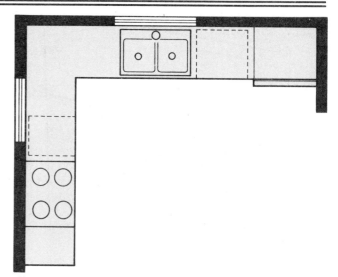

The L-shape is a common kitchen design and quite efficient where space is limited and no doorways intervene.

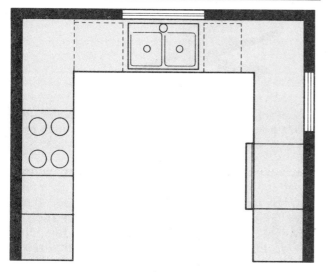

The U-shaped kitchen is the most desirable due to its high efficiency and maximum storage.

tion. The two legs of the L are on adjacent walls with no intervening doorways. This layout works well where space is limited; where there is a great deal of space, an island can be added or a peninsula extended inward on either leg to maximize efficiency.

The U-shaped kitchen is the most efficient, provides the most storage, and is the most desirable. The kitchen is arranged on three adjacent walls with a work center on each wall; often, the U can open onto eating or recreation areas or other activities. If an island or peninsula is added to an L-shaped kitchen, the layout can quickly be altered to the preferable U-shaped design.

A door within an L- or U-shaped layout transforms them into what is called a broken L or a broken U. Such broken layouts usually suffer a loss of efficiency due to through traffic.

Let us take a closer look at each of these kitchen layouts.

One-Wall Kitchen

In a one-wall kitchen, you do not have many choices regarding appliance placement, but you can put some flair into the layout.

The room should be a minimum of 14¾ feet long and 5 feet wide to conform with basic planning principles on counter space and appliance placement. A kitchen with at least those minimum dimensions allows for a sink area of 33 inches in the center; 36 inches of counter to the right of the sink as a food preparation area; 36 inches to the right of that area for the refrigerator; 24 inches for the dishwasher to the left of the sink; 30 inches for the range to the left of the dishwasher; and finally 18 inches of counter for work space and safety to the left of the range. The counters and appliances will protrude 24 inches from the wall, and you should allow at least another 36 inches—and that is truly a minimum—for movement.

The work triangle in this one-wall kitchen consists of a straight line measuring from the refrigerator at one end to the range at the other. This distance should not be extended any more than necessary even if the kitchen is longer than the one described. Extending the work triangle merely adds extra steps, and the amount of counter space provided in our example is certainly ample.

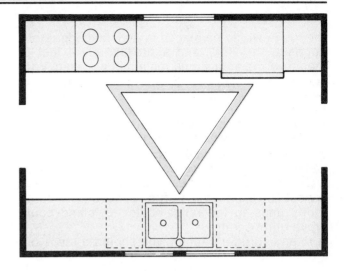

Traffic will cut through two legs of the work triangle when a corridor kitchen is positioned between other living areas.

If the room is smaller than the minimum, design principles go out the window and you must do the best you can. Fortunately, manufacturers of kitchen products offer several items to the person who must plan a one-wall layout in a room of less-than-minimum dimensions.

You can buy a compact kitchen—sometimes called a unit kitchen—that comes all in one piece. Compact kitchens are made of steel and are available in various colors. Frequently found in hotels or resort apartments, they combine a small under-counter refrigerator and a small sink with a small cooktop—usually two burners—that has a small oven underneath. They range in size from as little as 2 feet (acceptable only for a vacation home or as an auxiliary kitchen in, say, a recreation room) up to 6 feet and more. The all-in-one compact kitchen is not the only solution, however. There are a good many space-saving products that can help in a conventional kitchen that must be squeezed into a room of limited dimensions.

One firm makes a combination center that includes a cooktop with a dishwasher underneath and an eye-level oven above—all in a 30-inch space. Another manufactures a dishwasher that will fit under a shallow (6-inch bowl) sink. Ranges and refrigerators are also available in narrower-than-standard dimensions.

If the room is wider than 5 feet but narrower than the 8 feet required for a corridor kitchen, you can consider several options for increasing counter and storage space. Since wall cabinets are only 12 inches deep compared with 24-inch deep base cabinets, you could install a run of wall cabinets along the opposite wall in a room that is, say, 6 feet wide. Such cabinets can be ordered with the toekick, or they can be set on 2x4's recessed 4 inches and painted black. If additional work space is required, this run of wall cabinets can be topped with a countertop 13 or more inches deep. If you need additional storage space, you can either stack the standard wall cabinets to reach all the way to the ceiling or put in 84-inch utility and pantry cabinets that are no deeper than the wall cabinets.

Corridor Kitchen

The corridor kitchen utilizes two opposing walls. It is easy to install because there are no corners, and because it results in a maximum of counter space with a minimum of floor space, it is extremely efficient in terms of space utilization. It requires at least 8 feet of space between opposing walls, which leaves 4 feet of maneuvering space after the cabinets and appliances are installed.

If the corridor is positioned between other living areas of the home, a problem will exist with through traffic. Traffic will always cut through two legs of the work triangle, an unavoidable defect in this kitchen design that simply must be tolerated.

If the corridor is a cul-de-sac, the traffic problem will be lessened. With an eating or hobby area at the closed end, however, the traffic problem will appear once again.

If the corridor is more than 10 feet wide, you can solve any traffic problems by creating an island kitchen. The sink and refrigerator—with their countertop work spaces—would go on one wall,

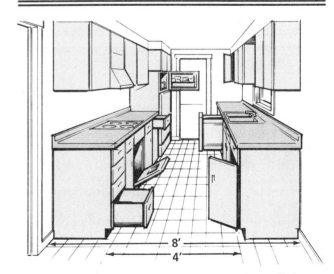

There must be at least 8 feet between opposing walls in a corridor kitchen for sufficient work space.

the range would be placed in an island (generally opposite the sink), and approximately 4 feet of maneuvering area would remain in between. With such an arrangement, it would be best to have at least 2 feet of counter space on either side of the range; assuming that you choose the popular 30-inch range, the island should therefore be 78 inches long and 24 inches deep. Standard base cabinets on either side of the range would provide valuable storage space, and you could use regular wall paneling to cover the back of the range since it would be exposed to traffic. However, extending utility lines to the range-equipped island could prove quite costly.

In any corridor kitchen, you should try to avoid placing the range and the refrigerator opposite each other. Situations in which it is necessary to have the oven door and the refrigerator door open at the same time could prove annoying.

L-Shaped Kitchen

An L-shaped kitchen involves turning a corner, and therefore it will normally be a little more expensive than a corridor design. However, it is a very popular layout, can be very efficient, and gives considerable latitude in appliance placement. Although an L-shape will not necessarily provide any more storage or work space than a corridor design, it does succeed in protecting the work triangle from cross-traffic.

The L-shape can be derived from two adjacent walls, or it can be formed by extending a peninsula out from a wall. A peninsula is often used when the room is large, especially when it can also separate the kitchen area from an eating or family activity area.

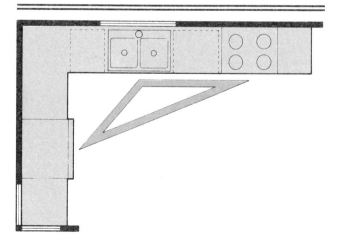

The range and sink usually go against one wall in an L-shaped kitchen with the refrigerator near the end of the other wall.

For efficiency and the saving of many thousands of steps, plan the appliances and work spaces so that they run sequentially from refrigerator to sink to range to serving area. The refrigerator usually goes against a wall at one end of the L.

The problem of turning the corner introduces opportunities for different design elements, some of which can waste space. The easy and cheapest way to turn the corner is with a blind base cabinet and a blind wall cabinet; a blind cabinet is one that has an unfinished part that butts against the side of the cabinet already in place. The butted area can vary by several inches—helpful in compensating for measuring mistakes. Unfortunately, there always will be a blind corner walled off from you by the cabinet walls.

In a blind base cabinet, you can get semi-circular shelves that are attached to the cabinet door and come out when you open the door. Such shelves are not available in a blind wall cabinet.

A better answer is frequently a lazy susan corner cabinet, available for base and wall. Some of these units have a corner door that opens to expose lazy susan shelves, while others have a pie-cut in the shelving to which doors are attached to form the corner. A push on the door in either direction spins the entire assembly around.

Another way to turn a corner is to design the sink or, less frequently, one of the appliances into the corner at an angle. Some double-bowl sinks are made in a pie-cut corner configuration, with one bowl placed on either side of the corner.

The main disadvantage to corner installations is that they consume a great deal of wall space. For example, a range that is 30 inches wide requires 45¼ inches of space along each wall of the corner. A 33-inch sink, placed diagonally, requires at least 42 inches along either wall. In addition, the space in the cabinet beneath is limited in its usefulness because you cannot reach all the way into it. This space can be utilized quite effectively, however, for sacks of potatoes or onions, dog food, or for waste container storage.

Assuming average appliances, a typical L-shaped kitchen would require—from left to right—36 inches for the refrigerator; 24 inches for the dishwasher (which automatically means 24 inches of countertop); 33 inches for the sink; 18 inches of counter before turning the corner; another 18 inches of counter before the range; then 30 inches for the range; and a final 18 inches of counter beyond the range. If a built-in oven and cooktop were being used, the cooktop could go in the same place as the complete range but there would be no good place for the wall oven until after the full run were complete. In other words, the wall oven would go at the opposite end from

Avoid crowding appliances into the L-shaped kitchen's interior corner.

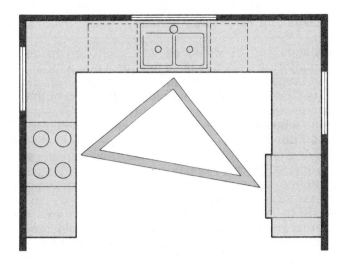

In a U-shaped kitchen, have 4 to 8 feet between the centers of the fronts of any two appliances.

the refrigerator, and thus add another 24 to 30 inches to the layout.

Try to avoid the tendency—very common with L-shaped kitchens—to crowd appliances close to the interior corner. Crowding almost always leads to unhappiness with the design.

U-Shaped Kitchen

A U-shape is the best, the most efficient, and the most popular kitchen design. It adapts easily to large and small rooms, and—with the basic appliances distributed on its base and two legs—it shortens the distances between the work centers.

The kitchen must be at least 8 feet wide at the base of the U (10 or 12 feet is preferable to avoid cramped working conditions), and each leg of the U must be long enough to accommodate a major appliance and the associated work space. A leg that will accommodate a refrigerator should be at least 4½ feet long; a minimum of 5½ feet long for a 30-inch range; and no less than 6 feet for the leg that contains the sink and dishwasher.

These dimensions are minimums, and while a U-shaped kitchen of minimum dimensions permits unrestricted operation of the appliances, it results in a cramped working area. For an efficient work triangle, try to have a minimum of 4 feet up to a maximum of 8 feet between the centers of the fronts of any two appliances. Since the U-shape works well in large kitchens without making the work triangle too long, kitchen designers often install a diagonal sink, a range, or a wall oven at the two interior corners.

Many U-shaped kitchens have long legs, often

flaring out into an eating area and often with one leg serving as a divider from another living area. Frequently, an eating counter is incorporated on one side of a long leg/divider.

When one of the legs serves as a divider between kitchen and dining or living room, the cabinets along that leg often open from both sides to give access from both rooms. Double-opening cabinets are available through home centers as well as from custom kitchen specialists. While the home center may not carry these cabinets as in-stock items, they can be ordered.

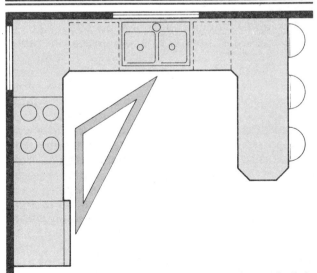

A peninsula that forms one of the legs can serve as a built-in eating area in a U-shaped kitchen.

Island and Peninsula Kitchens

Islands can be designed into a kitchen to add countertop work space, to provide a place for sink or range plus work space, to provide an eating area, or to provide something extra like a built-in barbecue or bar with hospitality center. An island can also serve to change a one-wall kitchen into a corridor kitchen.

A peninsula can serve as one leg of an L-shaped kitchen, one or two legs of a U-shaped kitchen, or create added counter space or eating area for any kitchen.

Both islands and peninsulas function well in large kitchens to make the work triangle more compact. In fact, the entire kitchen might be an island, with wall cabinets suspended from the ceiling. Two islands can be used to form a corridor kitchen in a large room, and one island might even form a one-wall kitchen in a large open area.

When the purpose of an island or peninsula is only to increase countertop space, either one need only be 18 inches deep from front to back. To add cabinets under an island or peninsula of this depth, you can put wall cabinets—the kind that are only 12 inches deep—on a kickrail; base cabinets are 24 inches deep and would not fit.

Normal island countertop depth is 26 inches. When a sink or range is to be installed in an island, though, this depth should be extended to 36 or even 38 inches to allow for spatter and splash.

Eat-In Kitchen

Most people like to have an eating area in the kitchen, ranging from a snack bar to full dining facilities.

For family dining, you must allow about 12 to 15 square feet per person to accommodate a table, chairs, and the people themselves. A family of four, for example, requires at least 48 square feet of floor space to accommodate a table and four chairs. Each adult needs 21 to 24 inches of table space, and you should allow a minimum of 36 inches of clearance between the table and a wall to edge around a seated person. A minimum of 32 inches is needed for a seated person to rise from a table, and serving around a table requires clearance of 44 inches from table to wall.

Snack counters along peninsulas or islands generally have the same clearance requirements for movement behind the chairs, and you still should allow 21 inches of space along the counter for each adult. By multiplying the number of people who will eat at the counter by 21 inches, you will arrive at the counter length you need.

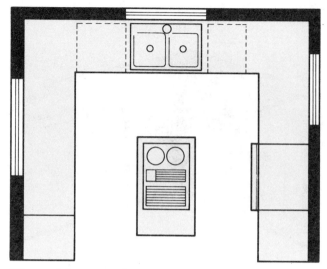

When a sink or range is incorporated in an island, the countertop depth of the island should be increased to 36 or 38 inches from the standard 26 inches.

The height of a counter used for eating need not be the same height as the kitchen work surface. A table-height counter will be 28 to 32 inches high; an eating counter the same height as the kitchen work counter will be 36 inches high. For the lower counter, a person will need 20 inches of legroom when sitting on a chair 18 inches high. For the higher counter, a person will require a bar stool with the seat 24 inches from the floor. With this

Allow 21 inches of space along a peninsula counter for each adult who will be eating there.

higher stool, required knee space decreases to 14 inches.

A high bar—more common when the eating counter backs up a sink or range center—will be 42 to 45 inches high. The height protects diners from spatter and splash, and it helps provide an open barrier from an adjacent living area. A standard high bar stool with a footrest will work well with the high bar.

When creating these eating areas, remember that the eating counter does not have to match the kitchen counter. It can be a contrasting color or pattern (a woodgrain top provides a rich look); at a different level; and it can be flared out, angled or circular.

EXTRA-ACTIVITY KITCHENS

A kitchen is often the focal point of home activities. Therefore, when planning a new kitchen design—assuming, of course, that sufficient space exists—give a good deal of thought to incorporating facilities for the extra activities that could take place there. Here are a few ideas:

• The family room kitchen. Your kitchen need not be a separate room. For example, you can create a kitchen at one end or on one side of a large living room/dining room. One-wall, corridor, L, or U kitchens are all possibilities, though the L- and U-shaped kitchens require plenty of open space.

The problems with the family room kitchen are few, but they must be considered. Ideally, housekeeping should be impeccable. Many people do not like to see open shelving or pot racks in a family room kitchen. Do not forget, moreover, that a family room kitchen means more noise and odors in the living area of the home than does a closed-room kitchen. The dishwasher, disposer, ventilating fan, and refrigerator all are souces of noise.

• The home office. The kitchen can be a convenient place for a home office, and facilities for an office can be designed into a kitchen quite easily.

An office in the kitchen calls for a dropped desk area with a counter about 6 inches below the regular 36-inch counter height. A desk should be at least 24 inches wide, with its depth matching the cabinet depth at that point. A single apron (shallow) drawer can be placed beneath the desk top, but it is essential that the drawer not interfere with knee space. A drawer unit or a two-drawer file can be placed beside the open knee space under the desk top.

If the desk area is positioned at the end of a cabinet run, an alternative to the drawer unit would be a narrow tray storage cabinet placed sideways against the wall. Again, it is essential that ample knee space be provided.

• The communication center. A complete intercom system—one that includes a two-way communication system between the kitchen and the bedrooms, recreation room, and basement; smoke and intruder alarms; radio and tape music facilities; and even a sophisticated closed-circuit TV for supervision of the children's play area can be installed in the kitchen. Such an installation should be located away from the work triangle.

• The craft and hobby center. The kitchen can provide a well-lighted area in the heart of the home for working on crafts and hobbies. Like the home office, the craft and hobby center that is incorporated in the kitchen may require little more than a cabinet or two suited to the activity, but if the hobby is one that requires a kiln or soldering or otherwise produces heat and fumes, an extra ventilating hood over the area should be installed.

• The greenhouse center. There are greenhouses made to fit in kitchen windows, and bulb manufacturers offer grow lights to help plants thrive. Such lights can provide a very pleasant lighting effect in the kitchen. Since kitchens develop special heat and humidity conditions that differ from other home areas, it is essential to consult an expert on the type of plants to buy for a kitchen greenhouse. Be sure to tell the expert whether your kitchen appliances are gas or electric; the difference is important when it comes to plant selection and care.

If you are into plants to any serious extent, you will need a place for potting, seeding, and transplanting. You can install a second sink in the kitchen—much like a vanity cabinet—and provide for seating or standing space around it.

The sink should have a gooseneck faucet and a spray attachment, and you will need open shelving or cabinets for pot storage and drawer for utensils. A pull-out or lean-out bin works well for soil storage.

Plants can be displayed in the kitchen window, on each side of the sink, or on an island or peninsula. They also can be hung from the ceiling. Be sure, though, that whatever surface is used for plant display is waterproof. Raw wood shelves deteriorate rapidly and therefore should be avoided in greenhouse installations. Plastic laminates are good surfaces and so are vinyls, especially when wrapped around the edges of the shelves.

• The laundry center. The best place for laundry facilities is not in the kitchen itself, but rather in a separate room adjacent to the kitchen. Washer and dryer units require about 5 feet of wall space, and they extend 27 to 33 inches out from

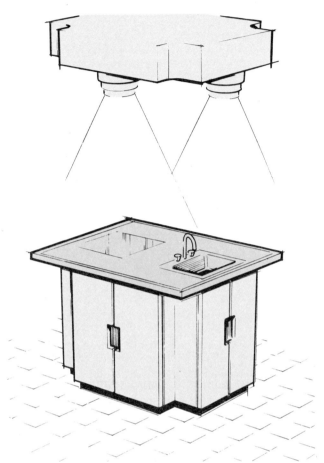

A kitchen hospitality center in a separate island can be equipped with a bar sink for preparation of drinks.

the wall, with space allowed for ducts and hoses behind. If possible, the dryer should be positioned against an outside wall for easy outdoor venting of the hot, moist air.

Cabinets for all laundry supplies must be in close proximity. A deep utility sink, plenty of counter space—at least 48 inches—and at least a 5-foot aisle for ironing space must also be designed into the laundry center.

• The hospitality center. The kitchen is frequently the place where drinks are prepared, and there is no reason—where space allows, of course—for not installing a bar. Since the bar should be well removed from the work triangle, the ideal place would be a peninsula separating the kitchen and living area. On the living area side, the peninsula could be equipped with a bar sink, and undercounter refrigerator and ice maker, liquor cabinet, and an overhead or side wine rack. It could also contain an indoor barbecue unit but such a unit would have to be adequately vented.

LIGHTING AND COLOR

Kitchen lighting must be planned from two points of view—decorative and functional. The decorative aspect depends not so much on the shapes of the fixtures, but rather on the way the light affects color rendition. As for the functional aspect, two types of illumination are needed—general, overall lighting, and localized lighting in work areas.

General daytime illumination is usually provided by windows. Some homes, however, are built with interior kitchens, where little daylight is available. In some cases, a skylight could be added to bring in daylight.

With daylight, window position has much to do with color rendition. North and east windows catch the morning sun, while those on the south or west get most of their light in the afternoon. Morning light tends to favor cooler colors like blues or greens. Afternoon light is kinder to warm red or earth colored tones.

Artificial light can be used to supplement daylight and to provide lighting at night.

Incandescent light is "warmer"—that is, it is more pleasing to skin tones, natural woods, and the color of food. The light always comes on immediately, can be readily hooked to a dimmer switch to control its brightness, and the bulbs or fixtures are less expensive. However, incandescent bulbs do generate more heat and consume more electricity, while putting out less actual light per watt than a comparably sized fluorescent tube. This kind of lighting source is best for the general dining area of the kitchen and for areas where food is prepared.

Fluorescent light is "cooler" in heat output and in color rendition. Compared to incandescent bulbs, fluorescent lighting is more energy efficient and produces about 250 percent more light for the current used; service life is about seven times that of incandescent bulbs. Fluorescent lights provide more even illumination with less glare, but there can be a slight flicker or hum (partially alleviated with diffuser panels and proper installation). Color rendition is "flatter" in the standard bulbs, though this can be eliminated by the use of warm white tubes that are designed to simulate the warmer tones of the incandescents. As a specific lighting source, fluorescents serve well as a general overall light in the kitchen and as specific "task" lighting over countertops and other areas.

One of the better ways to provide general illumination in the kitchen is to install a full luminous ceiling. This type of ceiling simulates natural daylight because it comes from above and in a broad source. It is important when such ceilings are installed that they are situated along the centerline of the room, with the tubes spaced at least 10 inches apart, and covered by diffusers, which spread the light and correct the flickering problem. Unless installed during new construction, however, luminous ceilings will drop the actual height of the ceiling in older homes. It will defeat the purpose of the illumination if the distance of the light fixtures to the diffusers is less than 15 inches; there will be shadows and the light will not be properly diffused.

Square or rectangular ceiling boxes with either tubes or bulbs that are surface mounted on the ceiling are also available. These boxes come in various sizes and are intended to replace the single fixture that is often standard general lighting in many homes.

Aside from a good source of general illumination, the well-planned kitchen should have directional or task lighting over the general work surfaces. Counter areas can be well-lighted by the use of under-cabinet fluorescent fixtures. Minimum length of such fixtures should be 12 to 18 inches. Use 15-watt tubes spaced about 30 inches apart.

Sinks that are beneath or near a window can be adequately lighted by one or two methods. Two 40-watt tubes mounted over a diffuser can be placed in the soffit or a 75-watt incandescent downlight can be centered over the sink.

Lighting requirements over a range are usually covered by the fixture built into the range hood. Typically, such fixtures take a 25-watt incandescent bulb or a 15-watt fluorescent tube; the latter should be the warm white type for the best color rendition. An alternative would be to use a recessed ceiling or soffit downlight with a 75-watt incandescent bulb focused down on the range top.

STORAGE IDEAS

There are times when a kitchen is too small for the things you want to put into it. A kitchen cabinet can make very efficient use of space; unfortunately, cabinets come in certain sizes that may not fit every situation. There are, however, other ways to take advantage of the smaller spaces commonly available in the kitchen.

One answer is open shelving. A wall cabinet is normally 12 inches deep, but you can get good use from shelving that is only 6 to 10 inches deep. One disadvantage to open shelving is that it requires attention and good housekeeping; dishes and other items that are on display must be kept clean and orderly. Hanging curtains in front of

the shelves can relieve cleaning to some extent.

Pot racks are another space-saver. Normally, they are suspended from the ceiling and can be used to hang pots, utensils, plants and other objects. However, these things, too, are on constant display and demand housekeeping.

Cabinet organizers are commercially available in many houseware departments. They fit inside cabinets and increase their storage capacity, making the space even more efficient.

Wall cabinets on an unused countertop can also provide additional space. Usually, such a cabinet is 12 inches deep, and if placed on top of a base countertop (normally 25 or more inches deep), it will leave at least 13 inches of usable counter space.

Peninsula or islands in the center of the kitchen can sometimes be added for extra storage or counter space. This can be especially useful in a one-wall kitchen where there is one long wall covered with cabinets. If all you require is more counter space, it can consist of a countertop only. Other alternatives include putting one or more wall cabinets beneath this or if you have the room, base cabinets below. There should be at least 1 inch of overlap of the countertops on all free sides.

Between-the-Stud Storage

Between-stud cabinets, which are designed to fit between standard wall studs, are available in different heights. Before installing them, check for pipes or electrical wiring behind the wallboard so that you have enough room to install the stud-cabinet.

You can cut out the wallboard in the area where the cabinet will fit with a keyhole saw. The cabinet will usually have a flange that will conceal any cut marks in the wallboard after installation. The cabinet is simply inserted into the wall and nailed from the inside into the two standing studs.

If you cannot find room to insert the cabinet into the wall, many units can be surface-mounted, although it may cause some movement problems.

Door Shelving

Door shelving mounts to the back side of a closet door and can be obtained in different sizes to accommodate shallow (can size) storage. You can, however, easily make such shallow shelving yourself from plywood and brackets, but do not make such shelving more than 4 inches deep or it will interfere with the operation of the door.

Drawer kits that enable you to put drawers in

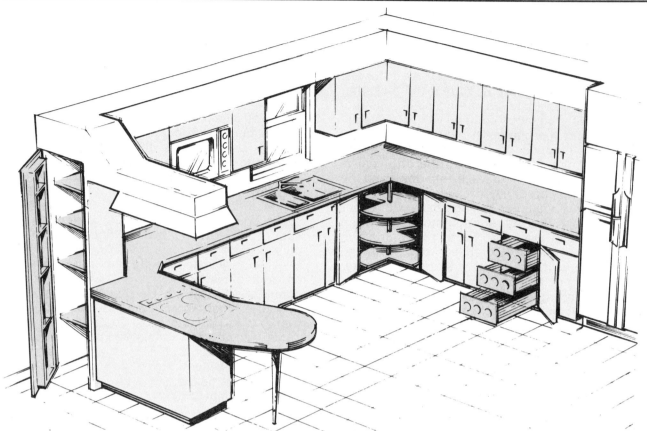

Typical kitchen installation showing some storage possibilities -- shelf storage in closet, Lasy Susan shelves in corner cabinet and hidden bread/produce drawers.

odd places are also commercially available. These are made to fit between standard studs; however, you should check the depth of the wall before buying any units. These kits also have brackets for installing drawers under a counter or into a wall. Most require at least 17 inches of space for the drawer clearance. If you have the room, they can be combined side-by-side or one under the other for a built-in appearance.

FINAL PLANS AND DRAWINGS

Before you actually begin remodeling, prepare a series of rough sketches that show all measurements and details. These can be refined sketches or informal drawings, but they should be done in considerable detail and preferably to scale. Of course, the larger the drawings, the easier they will be to work with. Be sure to include all the principal elements of the remodeling project, including wall placement; locations, types, and sizes of doors and windows; built-in furnishings, such as cabinets, counters, and shelves; and placement of plumbing fixtures and appliances. Note dimensions wherever necessary.

The plans can be prepared in a number of ways. A floor plan is the first requirement so you can work out proper placement and proportions of various elements. Interior elevations, which are simply detailed drawings of a single plane of the room as viewed head on, are also helpful.

Utilities drawings, such as those showing electrical and plumbing extensions, are usually drawn symbolically on a basic floor plan.

Do not skimp on details or specifications. The plans are designed to help you work out problems in advance and to serve as references as the job progresses.

As you work out the final plans, establish specifications for the materials, hardware, and equipment needed. You can note this directly on the plans or on separate lists. For instance, decide what type and brand of cabinets, floor covering, lighting fixtures and other materials you would like to have. Give these items careful thought to avoid time-consuming changes later. Make a list of all the items that will go into the project. This bill of materials should be checked against the plans or specifications lists several times to make sure nothing has been omitted.

Doing Your Own Kitchen

Once you have designed your kitchen, there still remains one problem: Who is going to do the work?

If you want a professional to do the job, the specialists in kitchen and bathroom remodeling are members of the American Institute of Kitchen Dealers, an association of over 1,200 professionals across the country who must qualify for membership. The cream of the crop of kitchen specialists are Certified Kitchen Designers; the initials "CKD" will be found after their names, corresponding roughly to the "ASID" of the qualified interior decorator.

Any kitchen furnishings' dealer will plan your kitchen, order the necessary materials, and arrange for their professional installation. He will usually offer a guarantee and the kitchen will be done in a minimum amount of time with as little disruption as possible.

Other groups include the National Home Improvement Contractors and the National Remodelers Association. While many of the members of these organizations are skilled in kitchen remodeling, their emphasis—for the most part—is on roofing, siding, insulation, dormers and the like; many do kitchen remodeling only as a sideline.

Before you sign anything, get references from the firm. Companies that are proud of their work will be glad to refer you to previous customers. Be sure the firm has a showroom and is not selling from a catalog. If the showroom does not have kitchen displays, you are taking a chance. And, preferably, the displays should show you both stock and custom-built cabinets, and built-in appliances as well as free-standing ones.

What you are looking for in a contractor is a solid business person who has an investment in the community, who pays taxes in the community, and who has a stake in it. When someone has invested thousands of dollars into a showroom, it adds to their credibility. As a last step, check the company with the Better Business Bureau.

You will pay for these professional services, and this cost factor can be prohibitive. An alternative, however, is for you to do some or all of the work. This can result in some substantial savings, in addition to the satisfaction you can have from knowing that you did the work yourself. There are, however, some things you should consider before assuming that you can do the work required.

MATERIALS

You can figure on paying about the same for materials no matter who does the final installation. While some dealers will give you a price break if you buy everything through them, it probably will not amount to any great saving. Rather than buying materials from one or two suppliers on a day-to-day basis, you might consider comparison shopping. Some possible sources include large hardware and supply discount houses, and cash-and-carry supply warehouses. Other potential sources for savings are special manufacturer's sales, sales on distressed materials and equipment, mill-end runs, obsolete or discontinued stock, warehouse inventory clearances, and materials or hardware auctions. You can also obtain good, used materials from various sources—and even buy leftover stock from building contractors.

Although this may all sound terrific, you do have to keep in mind that it is easy to get stuck. To be successful, remember three points. First, saving money this way requires ingenuity, judgment, and knowledge of building materials and their potential uses. You must know the difference—at a glance—between good-quality materials and hardware, and junk. Second, you must have a good grasp of standard retail prices of the materials that you wish to purchase. And third, buy only what you need, and pass up buying unnecessary items that seem to be real bargains.

Laying In Materials

Obviously, a certain amount of material must be laid in before you can start remodeling, but you must decide whether you want to buy all the materials before you begin, or whether you wish to have the materials arrive as needed. Both options have advantages and disadvantages.

If you have a clean, safe, and dry storage area, you may want to buy everything in advance. With such a major delivery, you may save money, and you may save time spent visiting suppliers and waiting for materials to arrive. And, you reduce the risk of a supplier running out of something just when you need it. This procedure also lets you view all the materials as a whole, and plan to make any minor adjustments due to irregularities in type or size. In particular, it is always wise to have all trim, specialty, and finish hardware items on hand. Then you can alter the construction specifics to suit them, rather than visa versa.

Stockpiling large quantities of materials, however, is not always the best course to follow. This is especially true if suitable storage facilities are not available, or if vandalism or pilferage is a problem. If your supplier maintains large stocks of materials, it may be best to buy only what you need for each few days' work, and let him take care of the storage problem. Also, buying materials only as you need them is a good idea when the project will be done bit by bit over a long period of time, but beware of a manufacturer discontinuing an item—hardware or paneling, for example, that you need to complete the job.

LABOR

In construction, material costs are typically smaller than labor costs. Kitchen remodeling is no different. If you do some of the installation work yourself, you may enjoy great savings.

If you are skilled and ambitious, you may want to do as much of the expansion work as possible by yourself. Some people may be able to tackle the entire project from start to finish, but most hire specialists for those parts of the job requiring special skills and equipment. It may boost your ego to say you did it all yourself. However, do you have the training or experience to do the job you want done?

Can you live with the long-term clutter and dislocation a large-scale do-it-yourself project will entail? You may be doing much of the work in your spare time, and this means that you will not be able to complete the whole kitchen for weeks, perhaps months. While you can schedule the work to suit your time (doing ceilings and walls one weekend, for example, and the floors the next), some jobs will require a much longer span. It will usually take an experienced carpenter at least a day to set a run of cabinets—in new construction. Older homes require more preparation and work. The walls are usually out of plumb, the floors may not be level, and there may be plumbing or electrical problems; the project will take longer to complete.

TOOLS

You must be familiar with tools and how to use them. The instructions in this book are based on the premise that you already know something about the general work at hand.

Before the project begins, all tools and equipment that will be needed—except rental tools—must be available and in good condition. If you already have a good selection of tools and know how to use them, this part of the job is easy.

An average-size home workshop usually contains all the basic tools needed to remodel a kitchen. You need a wide selection of carpentry tools: saws, hammers, measuring and leveling devices, drills and bits, squares, and screwdrivers.

Finish work calls for a miter box and saw, nailsets, planes, wood chisels and such. Power tools make the job much easier, and for most projects, you should at least have a portable circular saw and an electrical drill.

Do not attempt any major plumbing or electrical work unless you have experience in these areas! If you make a mistake and have to call someone in to rectify it, the cost may be more than if you had the job contracted out originally. Check your local codes; it may be mandatory for such work to be done by a licensed plumber or electrician, especially if it has to be inspected.

Basically, do-it-yourself labor in the kitchen comes down to time versus money. If you have the time and skill to do the job yourself; then by all means go ahead. You will save money and it will be fun to do something that you can take pride in for years (if you do it right, that is). It may be cheaper, however, to have somebody come in and do the more difficult chores.

The following do-it-yourself instructions are intended to supplement knowledge that you already have. They are not specific to any one particular kitchen.

Remove Existing Coverings

One of the first steps in remodeling is to remove existing interior finish coverings, sheathings, and trim. The job can be easy or ridden with problems, depending upon the circumstances. Here are a few suggestions that can make the job go smoothly.

TRIMWORK

Removing trimwork is the first, and probably the easiest, part of the demolition job. It must be done to clear the way for removal of structural framework, and can be done in a way that saves the material for reuse. Small moldings, like baseshoe, base, and quarter-round are best removed with a

wide, flat tool that can be used as a pry. A stiff putty knife or fine-bladed pry bar works well. A wide wood chisel sometimes works, but a screwdriver is much too narrow and blunt.

To remove a section of molding, start at a joint or at one end and cautiously work a bit of the piece free. Then, bow the piece out from its mounting surface. A slight amount of outward pressure is kept on it, and the piece is pried loose in a continuous movement toward a joint or the opposite end. The finishing nails that secured the molding should pull through with little trouble. If neither end of the molding is accessible, because the piece has two inside miter-cut corners, start in the middle and work in both directions. Moldings

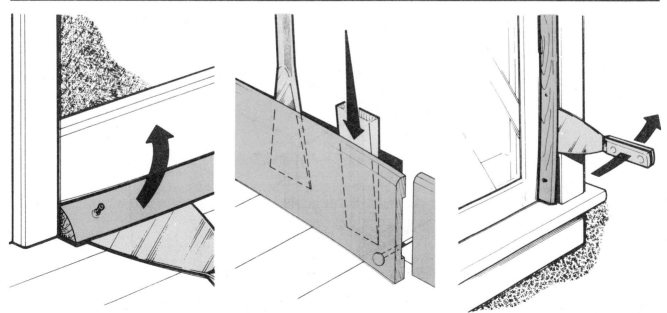

Three methods of removing trim are illustrated. Left: baseshoe molding can be removed with a wide-bladed putty knife. Middle: baseboard molding is best removed with a pry bar and wedges, working from one end to the other. Right: window casings can be removed like baseshoe moldings, with a putty knife.

covering a joint between a horizontal and vertical surface are frequently nailed to both surfaces, which makes removal more difficult. In this case, pick a likely looking spot and carefully work the piece free by joggling it outward; the nails should bend and finally pull free.

Flat trimwork—such as window or door casings, and baseboards—is easier to remove because it is stiffer, heavier, and less likely to break. Such pieces can be removed with a short, thin-bladed pry bar. Insert the blade under the end of a piece, rather than along its side. Jam the head of the pry bar against a solid surface, rather than against an unsupported expanse. Successive bites with the bar will free the piece.

When stripping a window assembly or other item with complex trim, the job will be easier if you first determine the original sequence of installation. Then start by removing the trim piece that was put on last, and work backwards through the sequence to the first piece installed. This reverse sequence method is also used for large trimwork, like box beams and boxed sills, which can be more difficult to remove. Usually the best course is to determine how and with what kind of fasteners the piece was installed. Then the process is reversed, starting with the last piece installed, and prying loose nailed pieces, removing hidden screws, and taking out bolts or lags.

Most trimwork is merely nailed in place, but occasionally some is glued. Depending on the quality of the job and the age of the glue, such pieces may not be removable without damage. You can

try to break the piece free with a wood chisel and mallet. Large trim pieces that were installed with screws, lags, anchors or other types of threaded fasteners, cannot be pried loose without ruining something. Try to find the fasteners and remove them first. Failing that, all you can do is rip and tear.

CABINETRY

Cabinetry and built-ins, of course, must be removed before any other major work can proceed. Prefabricated cabinetry that is purchased and installed as individual units is not usually difficult to remove. This is especially true if the units were separately secured with screws, lags, or anchors. In the case of wall-hung cabinetry, however, it is a good idea to jam plenty of props or supports beneath the units before removing the fasteners. This will prevent the units from falling free unexpectedly.

There are two types of built-ins. Some are built on site as units and then installed. Others are constructed piece by piece on location and use the house as partial support. It is usually easy to remove the former intact by locating and removing the fasteners. The latter, however, is almost always impossible to remove in one piece. All you can do, especially with the better kinds of nailed-and-glued construction, is to take off or take apart whatever pieces come loose easily, and break or saw the remainder into pieces. It is often difficult to salvage much.

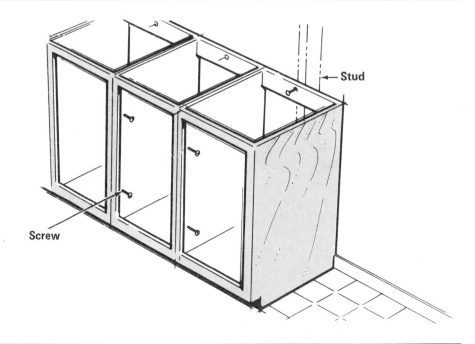

Remove screws and anchors in cabinets before attempting to dismantle.

Stud

Screw

CEILINGS

Tearing down old ceilings can be very unpleasant. There are only a few types that are likely to be relatively clean and easy to remove. One is the suspended-grid ceiling, which can be readily dismantled and salvaged entirely. The job consists of merely lifting the loose finish ceiling panels out of the gridwork, and removing any lighting troffers or other fixtures. Then the gridwork is disassembled by popping apart the snap-together sections. The wall-angle members, which are nailed in place, can be carefully pried loose.

Removing a tile ceiling is another easy project. If glued to a solid backing, remove the tiles by prying carefully with a putty knife. If stapled to wood strips, dig the staples out with a small-bladed screwdriver. The first few tiles will probably have to be broken out, but the rest can usually be saved.

Removing a drywall ceiling is a tough, dirty job, and removing a lath-and-plaster ceiling is a nightmare. Nothing can be salvaged, and the demolition is potentially dangerous. The usual inclination is to grab a wrecking bar and heave at it, but you could rupture a hidden water pipe or split a buried electrical cable. **Caution:** Before proceeding with any demolition, you should turn off the water and electrical systems, and locate pipes, wires, and ductwork, if possible. There is also a danger of getting struck by a falling or flying piece of material. Old plaster lath in particular is often tough and springy, and can snap apart or fly off with considerable force. Wear safety goggles to protect your eyes and be wary.

In addition, above-ceiling areas of older houses tend to accumulate a variety of debris—deep layers of house and coal dust, sawdust, mouse droppings, packrat nests, and other debris. Also, the older the ceiling, the more fine plaster dust it will generate during demolition. The result is a thick cloud of dust that can carry active germs, and act as a dangerous irritant, especially to people who have allergies or respiratory problems. Remember to seal all interior doors or door openings with tarps, and open all windows. Wear old clothes, long sleeves, gloves, a hat, a good dust respirator, and tight-fitting safety goggles. Change respirator filters often; wash your clothing and take a shower as soon as the job is over.

Old nails present a hazard, too. Chunks of drywall that come down will carry some nails, but many nails will remain in the framework. Plaster lath, however, usually comes away full of short and rusty nails. It is easy to step on one of these nails when your attention is focused on the work above. The best procedure is to keep the floor working area clear by moving rubbish to one side. If you do step on a nail or scratch or cut yourself, seek medical attention immediately.

Although unpleasant, the procedure for taking down a ceiling is simple enough. Remove all trim molding and lighting fixtures. Then find a likely spot out in the open and between joists and slam a hole through the material. From then on, it is just a matter of bashing and yanking until everything is down.

WALLS

Removing old walls is similar to ripping down ceilings, only easier. If the finish wall covering is plywood or hardboard paneling, you can probably salvage most of the material by carefully working the panels away from the wall studs or backing with a broad-blade pinch bar. Solid wood planking can be stripped away in the same way, although the first board or two is usually ruined.

As with ceilings, there is little hope of salvaging any material from drywall or plaster walls; they are just torn down in whatever way is handiest.

Before you knock down any wall, you must be sure to first strip trimwork, dismantle lighting fixtures, and remove convenience outlet covers. Also, turn off electrical power and watch for hidden water pipes and ductwork.

FLOORS

There is seldom much hope of saving any old flooring material, but it is usually not worth saving anyway. Except for plank-type flooring, removal is a matter of hacking, bashing, and prying up chunks of finish covering, underlayment, and subflooring, too, if necessary. Glued-down floor coverings, like tile and linoleum, can sometimes be loosened with a propane torch, *and* a great deal of caution. Then you can scrape down the underlayment and prepare it for a new covering. Wood strips or plank flooring can often be lifted piece by piece, by judicious use of a broad-bladed pry bar or chisel. Old wall-to-wall carpeting can simply be yanked free of its moorings. The underlayment or sheathing below is almost always suitable for recovering with new material.

One good method of removing old flooring in chunks is to use a circular saw, equipped with a special flooring blade. The blade is durable enough to withstand occasional nail hits. The circular saw's shoe is set so the depth of cut equals the thickness of the flooring. Then run a series of cuts in a rectangle or square, pry the cut section free, and go on to the next.

Cabinets

In rooms other than the kitchen, style is set by the furnishings, wall coverings and draperies. In the kitchen, it is the cabinets that set the style. They usually dominate the room merely because they cover such a large percentage of the walls. Cabinets, in a sense, are the kitchen's basic furnishings.

Aside from appliances, there is no category of kitchen furnishings where you will spend more money than on kitchen cabinets. If carefully selected and properly installed, good cabinets will last as long as the kitchen itself. Neither price nor appearance is a reliable indicator of cabinet quality. The significant factors are workmanship in the construction and the installation.

Style and design factors are a matter of personal choice. Apart from that, cabinets can be divided into three general categories. These are called stock, special-order, and custom. The main difference between the three is in cabinet construction. Price is not a good criterion. A top-line stock cabinet can easily cost more than a cheap custom model, and their appearance may be the same.

Stock cabinets are what their name implies: mass manufactured cabinets in a variety of standard sizes. Size is based on 3-inch standard

modules. The smallest is 9 inches wide, and each cabinet will be wider by 3 inches until the top width of 48 inches. Stock also means that they are kept in a warehouse for immediate delivery. What you are getting in stock cabinets is delivery convenience, a name-brand manufacturer, and a number of choices within preset limits. If a run of cabinets will not fit the available space, a stock filler strip will be used to make up the difference.

Special-order cabinets can be any standard size, shape, or finish. They are available with a wider choice of accessories than stock cabinets. A large manufacturer makes the cabinets to your order in the sense that the 'whole' kitchen is made at one time. They will still be a standard size box cabinet, but the finishes are sure to match exactly. For this service, you will pay a premium of 20 percent or more and there will usually be some delay in delivery. You will get a set of cabinets that will last, in the finish you desire, and with a fairly precise fit to the kitchen. Their general appearance will not differ substantially from stock cabinets.

Custom cabinets are usually made by a local craftsman within your area. The construction is different because the entire face frame of a run of

Cabinet Type	Do-it-yourself Installation	Durability	Cleanability	Do-it-yourself Repair
Wood				
Stock	Difficult	Good	Good	Fair
Special order	Difficult	Very good	Very good	Easy
Custom	Difficult	Good	Good	Easy
Printed finish	Difficult	Good	Fair	Poor
Laminates				
Domestic	Difficult	Excellent	Excellent	Difficult
Foreign	Difficult	Excellent	Excellent	Difficult
Steel				
Stock	Difficult	Excellent	Very good	Fair
Special order	Difficult	Excellent	Very good	Fair

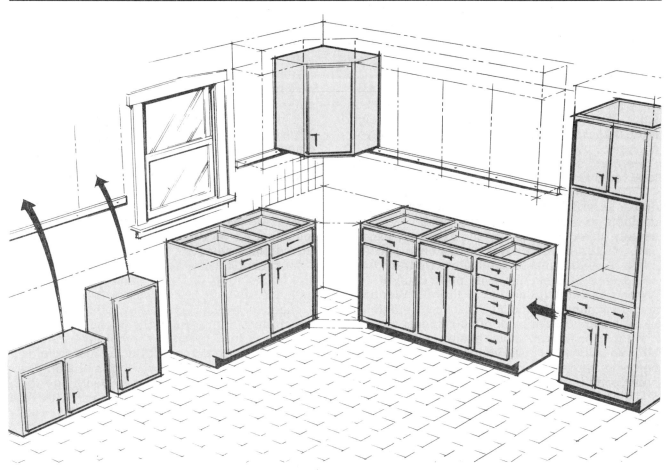

Typical layout showing where wall, base and oven cabinets fit.

cabinets is made in one piece and then the box built around that. You will get an exact fit to your kitchen and the spacing between the doors will be even for a uniform appearance. You will not get as wide a choice of additional accessories, nor will the finish be as good. The small craftsman cannot afford to stock the wide variety of accessories a large manufacturer can and his finishing line will not have as good a quality control system. What you are paying for is that 'built-on-the-job' look that only custom work can give you.

The difference between a good cabinet and a poor one is in materials and the workmanship. Here are some things to look for:

• Hardware, especially the interior parts of the cabinet. Drawer slides are important, because they are the main wearing parts of the system. Quality cabinets have metal slides; cheap cabinets have drawers sliding directly on the wood frame. The best drawer systems will feature double metal tracking with nylon and ball bearing rollers. Shelves should be removable, attached by

clips, and carefully constructed. All hinges should be strong, swing freely without binding, and be silent in their operation.

• Joinery, especially where stiles and rails (the vertical and horizontal framing) come together. The corners should be braced for dimensional stability. Drawers and shelves should be carefully put together with mortised joints. The whole box of the cabinet should look and feel sturdy.

• Materials. Solid wood is not the best material for certain purposes, because large pieces are subject to warping; if plywood is used, it should be a good grade and thick enough for stability. Cabinets with unfinished plywood shelves or flimsy backs are not recommended. Wide shelves should have support in the center to bear any expected weight.

• Style and finish are relatively unimportant, unless you choose a cabinet with a laminated surface. Laminates can splinter and their wearing qualities are only as good as the substructure beneath them. Molded or plastic drawers, for example, can break if a heavy weight is dropped in them. Any edges on laminated cabinets should be clean and neat, and the laminated surface as thick as possible.

• Steel cabinets are durable and easy to clean. They can also be purchased with a laminated or wood finish. One drawback is that they weigh more than wood, and this may be a difficulty if you choose to put them up yourself.

Here are some special buying tips you should look for when purchasing kitchen cabinets:

Take note of whether the manufacturer is domestic or foreign. Some dealers carry foreign cabinets as one of their display lines. These are usually of very high quality and extremely expensive. Most are in a contemporary style and finished in bright, plastic laminates. Delivery time could be a problem, however, particularly if you choose something unusual in fittings. Warranty service is generally good, but service is a definite question when buying imported cabinets.

Know something about quality cabinet construction when you make your selection. It may be better to spend a few dollars more on a special order cabinet rather than on a special offer the dealer may be having. Good cabinets are built to last and their price will reflect this.

Both knock-down and unfinished cabinets are available. The price differential in either case is only about 10 percent. With a knock-down cabinet what you are saving on is the shipping cost, but it takes time to design a good one of any variety and to build it. For uniformity of finish, only a large manufacturer can obtain consistent quality control, either in stock or special order work. Neither you nor a custom craftsman can afford the large finishing equipment necessary to do the job perfectly.

Carefully check the warranty on cabinets you plan to buy. While it is a federal requirement that all dealers just give you a set of installation instructions if you choose to do the work yourself, this may void the guarantee. Look for as long a warranty period as possible.

No matter what kind of cabinets you buy, they must all be installed correctly. The best cabinets will show 'racking' or other flaws if they are not set right. If you have any doubts about tackling this job, have it done by a professional.

CABINET STYLES

Since so much of a kitchen's styling depends on the cabinets, they should be selected prior to the flooring, wall coverings, and other items. All the other elements should then be chosen to harmonize with the cabinets.

What about the appliances? The most popular appliance color has always been white, and white will go with any style cabinets. Green and gold appliances require a bit more thought, but they generally blend in well with almost any cabinet color and woodgrain. One of the latest trends in appliance exterior design is the black glass front. More expensive than a painted surface, the black glass does blend nicely with any cabinet style.

One way to solve a possible—though unlikely—mismatch between appliances and cabinets is to add decorative fronts to the refrigerator, dishwasher, and compactor. These fronts are wood panels made by the cabinet manufacturer in a color and pattern that match the cabinets selected.

Most appliance manufacturers offer "front kits" consisting of metal frames that attach to their appliances. The frames are designed to hold a sheet of plastic laminate or other material to match the wood tones of the kitchen.

The four most popular cabinet styles are Contemporary, Traditional, Provincial, and Colonial.

Contemporary cabinet styling is characterized by straight, clean lines. Twenty years ago these cabinets were white enameled steel with flush doors and drawer fronts or flush overlay. Today, most contemporary cabinets have plastic laminate surfaces, many in bright solid colors.

Traditional styling usually features raised or recessed panels on drawer and door fronts. Normally quite conservative, traditional-styled cabinets are frequently made of oak in a wide color range. They can contribute to a look of elegance in the kitchen, especially in the more decorative versions.

Provincial is a fairly common style, characterized by a flat door with moldings applied to the faces of doors and drawers. French Provincial is noted for simple arcs in the moldings at the corners, while Italian Provincial has more complicated arcs and frequently some additional decorative touches as well. Common material for the Provincial styles is birch, although maple is also used as are plastic laminates in any color or woodgrain.

Colonial and Early American are theoretically two different styles, but cabinet manufacturers mix them so much that the two approaches represent variations on a common theme. In theory, a pegged, Early American board-and-batten door should never be called Colonial, while a raised-panel cherry door should never be called Early American. Colonial is a more rustic style, while Early American is always well-joined and finished. Knotty pine and maple are common materials for these styles. The board-and-batten look is

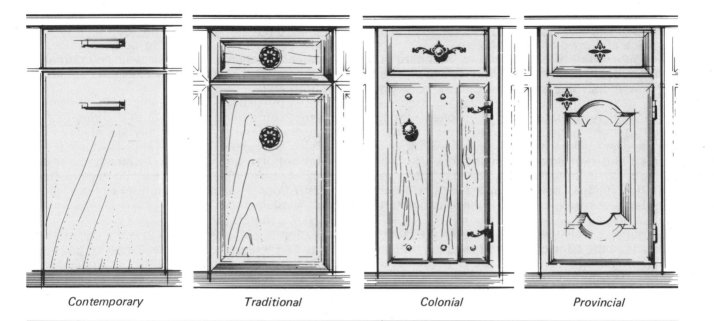

| Contemporary | Traditional | Colonial | Provincial |

achieved today by routing V-grooves vertically on the doors and horizontally on drawer fronts—randomly or with even spacing.

There are also many special styles achieved through the use of colors, graphics, wood carvings, and other decorative techniques. Manufacturers offer cabinets with hand-rubbed tints—light blue, for example—that allow the woodgrain to show, while paints and decals can create a mod or graphic theme.

Style, of course, is a matter of personal preference, and no particular style is inherently superior. Just remember that cabinets must be chosen either to complement a theme or to remain essentially neutral. For example, an elegant Traditional style cabinet would hardly go well in a kitchen emphasizing a Provincial or Colonial decorative theme.

CABINET TYPES AND SIZES

Kitchen cabinets come in a variety of types and sizes to suit various storage needs.

Wall cabinets are generally mounted on the

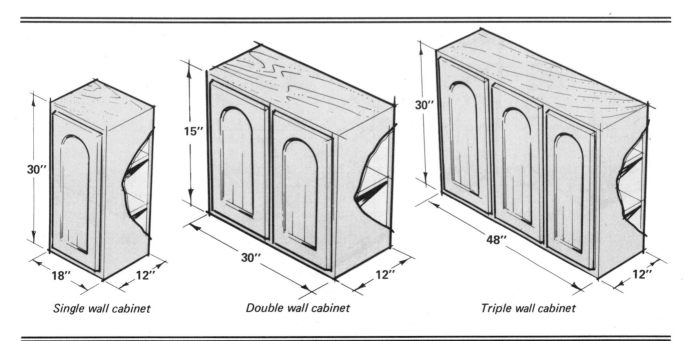

Single wall cabinet   Double wall cabinet   Triple wall cabinet

walls, although they can be hung from the ceiling over a peninsula or island; they can even be put on a toekick and used as base cabinets.

Although wall cabinets are a standard 12 inches in depth (with the doors projecting an extra ⅜ to ¾ inch), they can differ greatly in height. Those 12 to 15 inches high are usually mounted above high refrigerators and high oven ranges, while 18-inch models are used over standard ranges, over the sink (when there is no window, of course), and over smaller refrigerators. The wall cabinets 30 inches high are the basic storage units for dishes, glasses, and foods. Custom manufacturers frequently offer these cabinets in models reaching 32 or 33 inches high.

Diagonal corner cabinets are also 30 inches high, as are the blind corner wall cabinets that are useful in turning corners in an L- or U-shaped kitchen. Diagonal corner cabinets can be fitted with regular or revolving shelves.

Peninsular wall cabinets for use over the range or sink are generally 18 inches high, while those for storage are 30 inches high and frequently open on both sides for easy access to stored items. They are usually hung from a soffit.

The other basic type of kitchen cabinet is the base cabinet. Base cabinets are 24 inches deep and 34½ inches high, including the toekick, which measures 4 inches deep and 4 inches high. Base cabinets are used for storage.

As with wall cabinets, base cabinets are available in diagonal corner, blind corner and lazy susan corner units for turning corners in L- and U-shaped kitchens. Like their wall counterparts, peninsula base cabinets may have doors opening on both sides.

While the usual base cabinet has one drawer at the top, some consist entirely of drawers (called base drawer units); they usually are placed near the sink and range. Under the sink itself is either a sink front or a sink cabinet. The sink cabinet is a complete box with a floor and back; the sink front has no floor or back (although an optional floor can usually be obtained).

Oven cabinets are tall cabinets used for installation of wall ovens. Available in stock sizes of 24 or 27 inches wide and 84 inches high, oven cabinets are designed for either a single-cavity oven or a double oven.

Tall utility cabinets reach up to 84 inches high. Usually 18 or 24 inches wide, they can be used for various storage needs (mops, brooms, cleaning supplies, etc.) Fitted with adjustable, revolving or fold-out shelves, these cabinets can also function as pantries for bulk food storage.

When a run of cabinets fails to fill a given space, manufacturers offer wall and base fillers to fill in the odd dimensions. Fillers can also provide clearance for drawers in a corner, render a decorative termination to a cabinet run, etc. Just

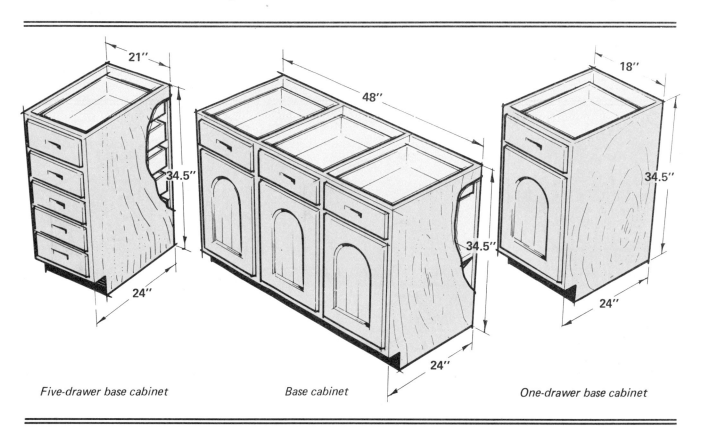

Five-drawer base cabinet   *Base cabinet*   *One-drawer base cabinet*

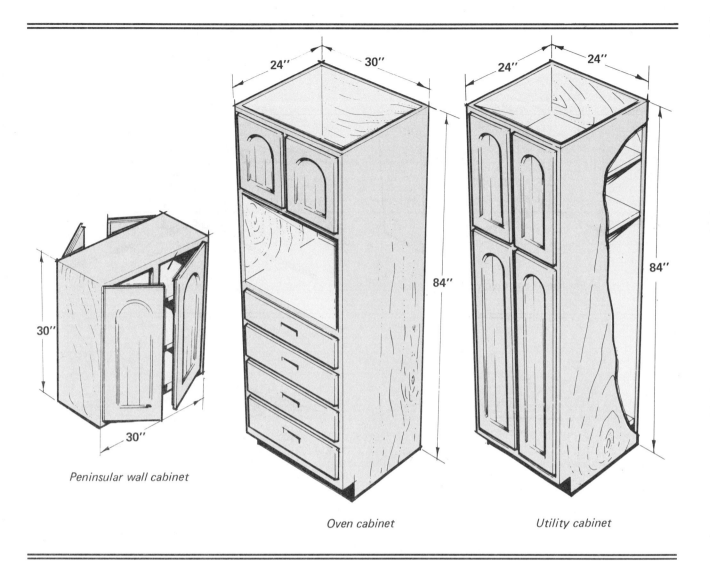

Peninsular wall cabinet

Oven cabinet

Utility cabinet

how many and what type of fillers are needed depend on the size and style of the kitchen.

HOW TO INSTALL KITCHEN CABINETS

Kitchen cabinets must be installed with painstaking care, and that's not easy. Cabinets are usually installed before final finishing of the floors and walls and laying of finish floor material. They are permanently installed by securing them to the structural framework. The floor must be prepared so it is reasonably level, and the walls where the cabinets will be mounted must be made so that they are as close to perfectly plumb as possible. Any high or unshimmed low spot on the wall or floor can cause racking of the cabinet, which will force the drawers and doors out of alignment.

The most expensive cabinets cannot compensate for improper installation. If poorly installed, the best cabinets will work no better than the cheapest.

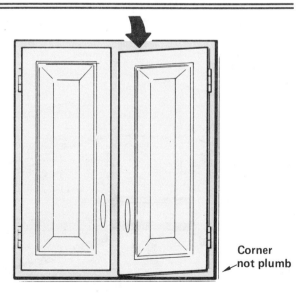

Corner not plumb

Unleveled cabinets can cause racking.

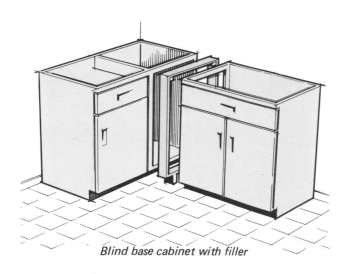

Blind base cabinet with filler

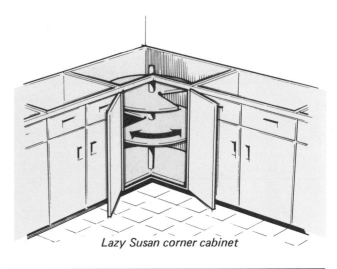

Lazy Susan corner cabinet

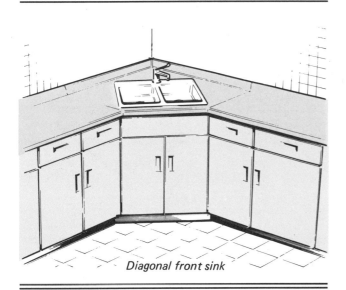

Diagonal front sink

Pie-cut corner sink

Recessed corner oven

Diagonal corner oven

The above illustrations show many different ways of turning a corner.

Before you start, equip yourself with the following items: one or two helpers; a 1x2-inch strip of wood (to use as a cleat to help support wall cabinets); an electric drill with a ⅛-inch bit and a 90-degree drilling adaptor; a 4-foot level; a screwdriver; a T-brace (made from a 54-inch length of 2x4 topped by a 1-foot piece of 2x4 mounted at right angles and covered with carpeting); a box of 2½ inch No. 10 wood screws; a couple of C-clamps; wood shingles for shims; and a box of toggle or molly bolts.

When you have everything you need—including, of course, the cabinets—follow these instructions:

Make sure your electrical and plumbing rough-in is complete. Then carefully examine your design drawings, familiarizing yourself with just how the base and wall cabinets are supposed to run.

Prepare the room. Shave or sand down all obvious high spots in the walls.

Locate the wall studs behind where the cabinets will be, and mark their location on the wall. Although the distance between studs—center to center—should be 16 inches, you cannot rely on that standard distance, especially in older homes. Therefore, be sure to mark the location of every stud along the run, placing the marks both above and below where the cabinets will be; you will want to be able to see the marks after the cabinets are in position.

Move all the cabinets, still in their boxes, to an adjacent room where they will be handy but will not interfere with your work. Check your drawings once again, and then number the boxes and the appropriate wall locations to make sure you get the cabinets in the right places. You should start installing from a corner, and you should mount the wall cabinets first to avoid damaging the base cabinets. Therefore, arrange the cabinets in the adjacent room in a way that makes for an easy and orderly flow into the kitchen.

Attach the 1x2-inch strip to the wall precisely so you can rest the bottom back of each wall cabinet on it when you move the cabinet into position. For standard 30-inch wall cabinets, the top of

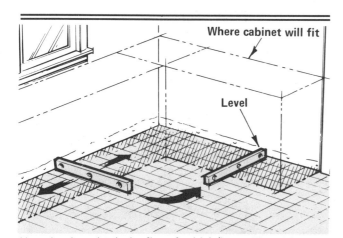

Use a level to check the floor for high/low spots.

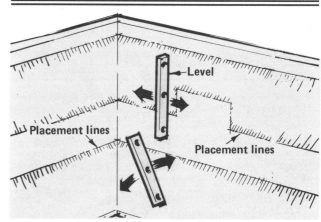

Use a level to check the walls for high/low spots.

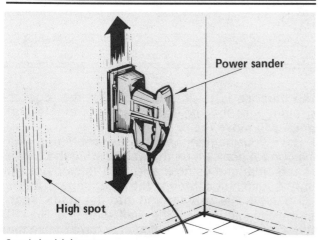

Sand the high spots.

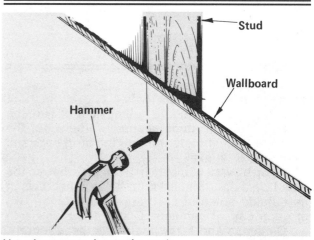

Use a hammer to locate the studs.

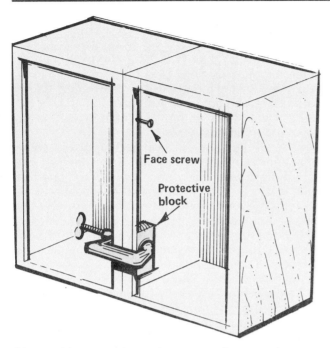

Clamp cabinets together and screw together securely.

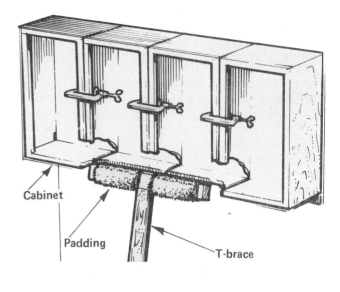

Use T-brace to help hold wall cabinets while fastening.

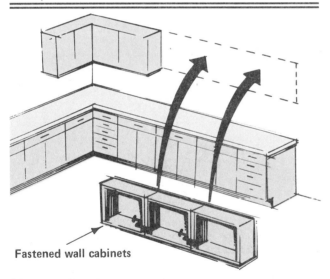

Line up wall cabinets as one unit.

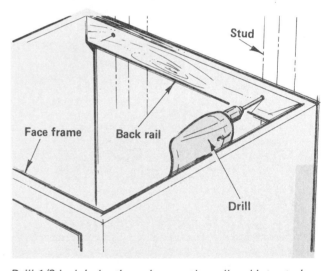

Drill 1/8-inch holes through mounting rail and into studs.

the cleat should be 54 inches above the floor (assuming a 8-foot floor-to-ceiling height). Nail the cleat to the wall studs securely (otherwise, the weight of the cabinets will pull the strip out), and make sure it is level.

Line up all wall cabinets in a run together on the floor. Use a drill to make pilot holes for screws in the outside stiles of each adjacent cabinet; two for each pair of cabinets. Clamp the stiles with two C-clamps and screw them together securely.

The purpose is to line up all faces in one level, straight run, making the cabinets a single unit when you move them.

Have your helpers hold up the whole unit into the correct position on the wall, resting the backs on the cleat and using the T-brace to help hold it. Drill 1/8-inch holes through the mounting rail at the top back of the cabinet and into the studs. Then screw the cabinet to the wall with the No. 10 screws, four per cabinet. You may have to use the

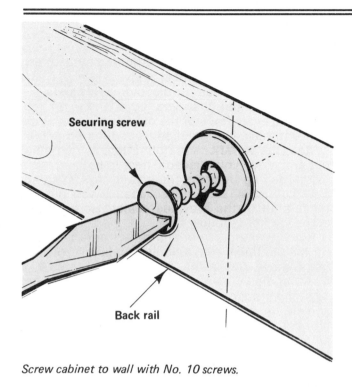

Screw cabinet to wall with No. 10 screws.

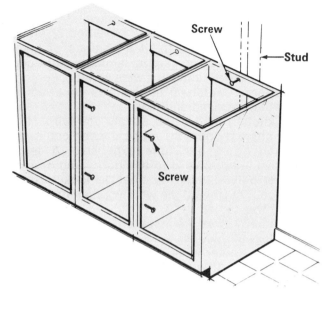

Fasten base cabinets together as a unit and fasten to wall.

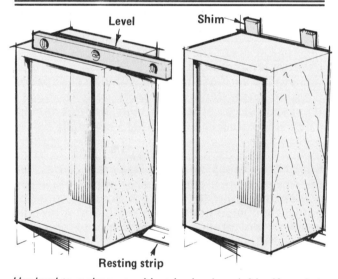

Use level to make sure cabinet is plumb and shim if needed.

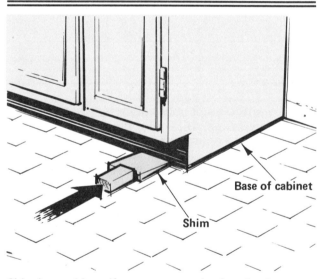

Shim base cabinets if necessary to make them level.

toggle bolts if there are not enough available studs.

Check the assembly with a level to make sure it is plumb, and do whatever shimming is needed before tightening the mounting screws.

Follow the same basic procedure with the base cabinets; fastening them together as a unit and then moving them against the wall. You will not need a cleat or T-brace for the base cabinets; but make certain the whole unit is shimmed level so that a countertop will rest securely.

When you finish installing all wall and base cabinets, insert the drawers, hang the doors, and attach appropriate hardware.

HOW TO UPGRADE OLD CABINETS

If your present kitchen cabinets are sound, solid, and agreeable in terms of styling, there is no need to replace them just because the finish is flawed.

You can replace doors and drawer fronts no matter whether your cabinets are wood or steel. One system designed to fit all brands of steel cabinets consists of plastic laminate surfaced doors and drawer fronts in a wide variety of colors and patterns. Matching laminate is supplied to cover other exposed surfaces.

Any kitchen dealer can supply you with high quality custom doors for your old wood cabinets, but such doors are quite expensive. A less-expensive alternative is to use doors and drawer fronts of polyurethane, finished to look exactly like wood. You can do the work yourself or have it done by the dealer.

When new doors are installed, very little of the old cabinet surface is exposed. Most people simply apply a darker varnish over the exposed face frame because it will not make a sharp contrast with the new doors. Larger exposed surfaces—an end panel or the sides of wall cabinets framing windows—can be covered with panels that match the doors.

The cost of this replacement customarily runs less than half that of replacing cabinets, if you have the work done professionally. If you replace the doors yourself, the price would be only about 25 percent of full cabinet replacement.

Painting

If you want to paint your cabinets, you can do so effectively with a solid-color paint, either a gloss or semi-gloss enamel. You need enamel to provide moisture-resistance.

The cabinet surfaces must be clean and smooth before painting, but it is not necessary to remove the old finish. Just sand rough spots to smooth finish, and wipe the surface clean. Make sure the surface is dust free. Then paint the cabinets as you would any other wooden surface.

Refinishing

If you prefer to keep the natural finish of the wood visible, you can refinish your cabinets, but the job is much more complicated than painting. Simply stated, refinishing cabinets is an exhausting task if done properly. It can require many days, even weeks, if you have a large number of cabinets in your kitchen. Opting for a professional refinisher to come into your home and refinish your cabinets ·is a possibility, but having such work done for you is extremely expensive.

If you decide to do the work yourself, plan on carrying out bucket after bucket of stripper and the liquefied old finish. Be sure to cover and protect all areas on which the stripper could splash or drip, and wear rubber gloves because the chemicals could burn or discolor your hands.

It is essential that you do a thorough job, removing every trace of the old finish. Look at the area you have just finished from different angles so that the variations in light intensity can point out any areas you missed. There is nothing more disheartening than watching your new finish appear "blotchy" as it dries because you did not remove all of the previous sealer. Here are the steps you must follow:

Remove the drawers and door fronts and take off the old finish with a liquid stripper. If you cannot remove the doors and door fronts, use a heavy-bodied cream remover because you do not want the stripper running off the surface and onto something it could damage. With either type of stripper, be sure to follow the instructions on the label. If your cabinets are constructed of open-pore woods—such as oak or walnut—scrub the surfaces repeatedly with steel wool dipped in the finish remover.

When the old finish is gone, clean off all traces of the remover with lacquer thinner or mineral spirits. If traces of the remover remain on the surface of the wood, they will cause the new finish to become blistered or patchy.

Sand the surfaces by hand with fine sandpaper. If you discover dents or nicks in the finish, repair them with wood filler and then stain to match. Allow these treated areas to dry thoroughly before proceeding.

With open-pore woods, brush on a liquid wood filler both across and with the grain. When the filler dries (it will appear hazy), wipe with a rag across the grain to force the solution into the pores; then wipe lightly with the grain. Allow the wood to dry at least 8 hours before going to the next step.

If you wish to stain the wood, now is the time to do it. Follow the directions provided by the manufacturer of the stain.

Seal the surface of the wood with shellac or a name-brand wood sealer. Apply two coats (via brush or spray) sanding lightly between coats. Once again, follow the instructions on the label.

Now give your cabinets a protective coat of resin varnish or lacquer. Remember, two thin coats are preferable to one heavy coat. Be sure to avoid drips, runs and brush marks in this final finishing procedure.

After the finish has dried sufficiently—one or two days—wax with a preparation containing carnauba wax. Do not use a liquid polish. Buff the finish to a deep, lustrous sheen.

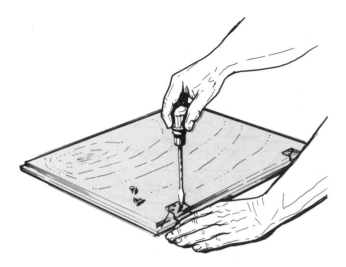

Remove all hardware from the doors.

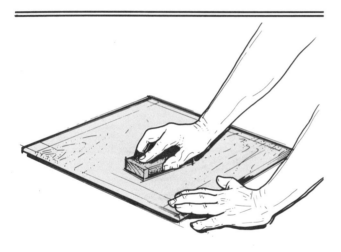

Sand surfaces by hand with fine sandpaper.

Resurfacing

Resurfacing old cabinets represents another popular alternative to the expensive task of installing new ones. Firms that do cabinet resurfacing come to your home, remove the old doors and drawer fronts, and take these parts back to the shop. They sand the doors and drawer fronts, and then apply new surfaces of plastic laminate. When the resurfacing work is completed, they bring the cabinet parts back to your home and remount them. Face frames and other exposed surfaces can be laminated in your home to match the doors and drawer fronts.

If you opt for this procedure, you can choose from more than 100 woodgrains, patterns and colors. You can even have the fabricator rout Provincial-style or V-grooves (to simulate board-and-batten) in the doors or have him apply moldings to create a Traditional or Colonial style.

Be sure the fabricator applies laminate to both sides of the doors. You can have the same pattern on both sides or select a less-expensive backer sheet. But you need the laminate on both sides to balance the door and thus prevent warping. An uncovered back could cause the door to bow out in front.

One of the easiest ways to resurface old cabinets and to give them an entirely different look is with durable vinyl panels available from a number of manufacturers. The panels, which are very resistant to stains and scratches, come in a variety of sizes that can be fitted to any cabinet door or drawer front. Matching material is available to fit rails, stiles, and other surfaces.

In addition to the vinyl panels, you will need a screwdriver, sanding block, ketone solution for cleanup, a ruler and a marking pencil, utility knife, contact adhesive with spreading brush, wax paper, a small paintbrush, and a trim paint in matching color. Here are the steps to follow in do-it-yourself cabinet resurfacing:

Remove the old doors, and then take off all the hardware (pulls, hinges, etc.). Sand the door surfaces until they are smooth. Wipe the surfaces clean with ketone.

Measure the doors, and mark the dimensions on the panels with a pencil.

Trim the panels to size with a utility knife.

Apply contact adhesive to the backs of the panels and to the fronts of the doors. Allow the adhesive to become dry to the touch—usually about 15 minutes. At this point, the adhesive will not feel sticky, but it will grab another adhesive surface.

Lay wax paper over about ¾ of the door (it won't stick), and very carefully position the panel over the door on the wax paper. Don't let the panel and door touch because the two will adhere instantly and be very difficult to adjust. When the portions separated by the wax paper are perfectly positioned, press down all over. Then pull out the wax paper and press once again.

Paint the edges of the door with the matching trim paint.

If any surfaces of the face frame are exposed, paint them or apply flat strips to cover them in the same way you did the doors.

When the paint is completely dry, rehang the doors.

Wipe door surface with ketone.

Apply contact adhesive to back of panel and front of door.

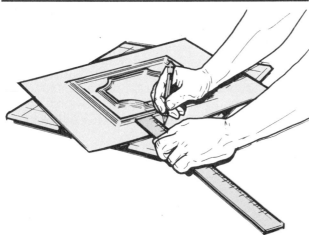

Measure doors and mark dimensions on panels.

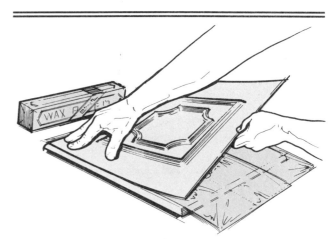

Lay wax paper over about 3/4 of door and carefully position panel on the wax paper.

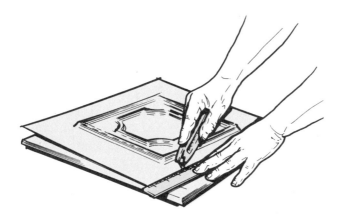

Trim panel to size with utility knife.

Paint edges of door with matching trim paint.

Countertops

Thinking about replacing your countertop? If so, you have a choice of four basic materials: high-pressure plastic laminate, Corian, ceramic tile, and laminated hardwood.

High-pressure plastic laminate is the least expensive and by far the most popular kitchen countertop material. It comes in a tremendous range of patterns, colors and woodgrains. As countertop material, it usually is 1/16 of an inch thick, although identical material 1/32 of an inch thick is available for use on vertical surfaces or table tops; the thinner type should not, however, be used on kitchen countertops. You can buy high-pressure plastic in sheets and laminate it yourself to 1½ inch plywood or particle board, but it is far easier to buy prelaminated boards ready for countertop installation.

Corian is a DuPont synthetic marble that differs from other artificial marbles in that it is drillable, cuttable and can generally be worked like wood. However, it is heavy and care must be taken because it chips readily. Considerably more expensive than laminates, Corian is a superb material for a kitchen countertop. You can even buy a Corian top with an integral sink bowl of the same material, all in one piece. If you install it yourself, put in the ¾-inch thick Corian, using the ¼-inch thick material for the countertop backsplash.

Ceramic tile is the most expensive countertop material. Very popular on the West Coast and throughout the Southwest, it is elegant and very durable, but it has some disadvantages too. Its very hard surface tends to reflect noise, and the grout between the tiles can pose a cleaning problem if it is not sealed properly. Tiles range in thickness from ¼ to ⅜ inch and in size from a ½-inch to a 6-inch square. The 4¼ inch square is regarded as the most popular.

Laminated hardwood is the familiar butcher block material. Always popular on a limited scale—particularly for the food preparation section of the countertop—butcher block has been used throughout many kitchens. The hardwood involved usually is maple; thickness can vary, but the 1½ inch material is quite common. The wood must be well sealed to prevent excessive staining, and it requires a good deal of care and attention to look its best.

To enhance the flexibility of your new countertop, consider including special-purpose inserts.

Material	Do-it-yourself Installation	Durability	Cleanability	Do-it-yourself Repair
Laminated slab				
Post-formed	Fair	Very good	Excellent	Poor
Self-edged	Fair	Very good	Excellent	Poor
Custom	Fair	Very good	Excellent	Poor
Corian				
¾ inch	Difficult	Very good	Excellent	Excellent
½ inch	Difficult	Very good	Excellent	Excellent
With integral bowl	Difficult	Very good	Excellent	Excellent
Ceramic Tile	Fair	Excellent	Good	Fair
Butcher block	Fair	Poor	Fair	Poor

The inserts most often used are butcher block, but an increasingly popular material is Pyroceram, a tempered glass ceramic that will not cut, stain, or scratch. Stainless steel inserts are sometimes used, but stainless steel dents, dulls knives, and scratches.

HOW TO INSTALL A PLASTIC LAMINATED COUNTERTOP

Plastic laminated countertops can be self-edged or postformed. Self-edged tops have a square front and are faced with a separate strip of the same material found on the top. The backsplash is a separate piece joined at right angles to the top. In contrast, a postformed countertop is rounded over the front edge (often raised there for a "no-drip" top) and coved up at the backsplash and over the top to the wall.

Plastic laminated countertops are available in 6, 8, 10, and 12 foot lengths. If two lengths are to be joined to form an L, they must be joined with a 45-degree miter joint. Your dealer can cut the miter for you, and you can put the two pieces together in your kitchen.

To install a plastic laminated countertop, you will need the following tools: a screwdriver, hammer, small wedge, level, tape measure, some ¾-inch stock, nails, adhesive caulking, a pencil, wood screws, a drill and drill bits, transparent tape, and—if there is a miter joint—an adjustable wrench to tighten bolts.

To replace an existing countertop with a plastic laminated postformed one, follow these instructions:

Remove the old countertop. Since it probably is fastened to the base cabinets with screws, check inside the base cabinets for screws or nails. Remove the fasteners, and then lift off the old top. Be careful, though, because in addition to screws or nails, the countertop may be glued down, and pulling it up sharply could damage the base cabinets. A hammer and wedge may be necessary to free a glued countertop.

If necessary, level the base cabinets by shimming them at the floor.

Place the new top in position, and then measure up from the floor. The top surface should be 36 inches from the floor to provide clearance for under-counter appliances and drawers. Most countertops need to be raised to this height. Turn the top over and nail ¾-inch thick, 2-inch square blocks along the front and back, spacing them about every 8 inches. Use nails no longer than 1⅛ inches; longer nails could penetrate the top.

Assemble the miter joints by placing the sections together—bottom side up—on a soft sur-

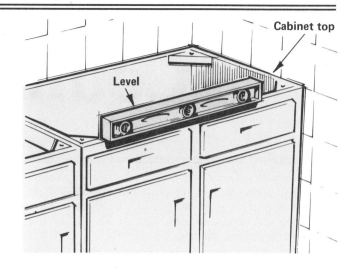

Use level to check cabinets.

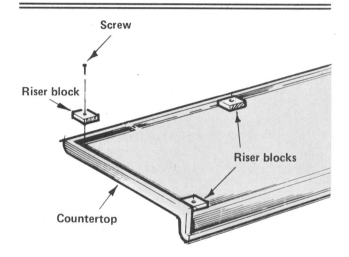

Install riser blocks under countertop.

face that will not damage the countertop. Apply an adhesive caulking compound to the surfaces to be joined, and then use fasteners (I-bolts should come with the top and fit into special slots) to hold the sections together. Turn the fasteners snug but not tight. Check alignment of the front edges and top surfaces, and then tighten the front fastener. Now check again, and then tighten the next fastener. Follow this procedure until all the fasteners are tightened. When you turn the bolted sections over and clean off the excess caulk, you should have a perfectly formed miter joint.

Push the postformed countertop back against the wall (or walls if an L). Then take a pencil, place it vertically against the wall with the point on the backsplash, and draw a line all along the top of

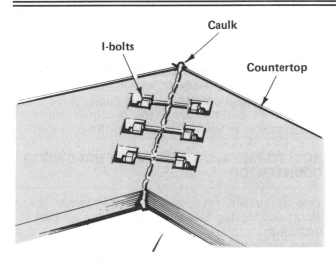

Bottom view of miter joint.

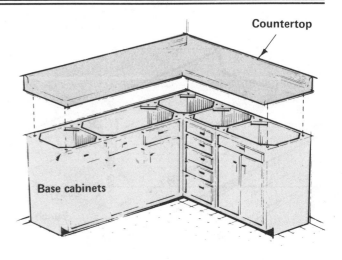

Fit countertop to cabinets.

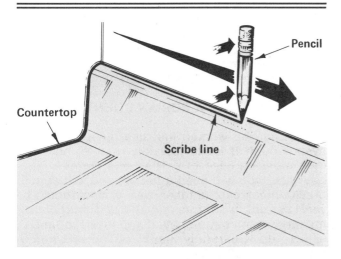

Scribe line to check countertop fit.

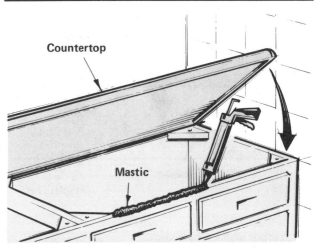

Glue countertop to base cabinets.

the backsplash. If this line bows out, you know where you must file or sand away a little of the backsplash so that the countertop will fit flush against the wall. File and sand the backsplash until it fits flush.

Fasten down the top with wood screws through the triangular gusset plates in the corners of the base cabinets. If your cabinets do not have gussets, you should have wood blocks in those corners through which you can drill holes for screws to hold down the four corners of the countertop. If you are certain that you will never want to remove the countertop, you can apply panel mastic—put on a continuous bead running around the entire perimeter—to hold the top in place.

For a sink installation, check the sink carton for installation instructions and a template for making the sink cutout in the new countertop. With a keyhole saw, you can make the cutout from the top; with a saber saw, you have to cut from the bottom or the laminate will chip. Using the template, draw the line for the cutout. Use a sharp punch or nail inside each of the four corners to make pilot holes for the drill, and then drill holes all the way through at each corner. Be sure the bit does not cut outside the guideline, and be sure before you cut that you have spaced the sink properly from front to rear so that there is room for its rim in front of the backsplash.

Start sawing from hole to hole with the keyhole saw. To avoid chipping the laminate, apply transparent tape over your cutout line. If you use a keyhole saw do not saw too hard; apply pres-

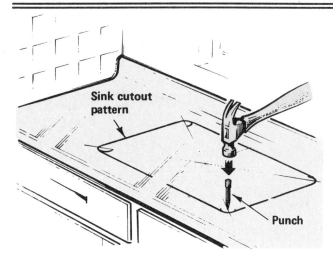

Make pilot holes for drill.

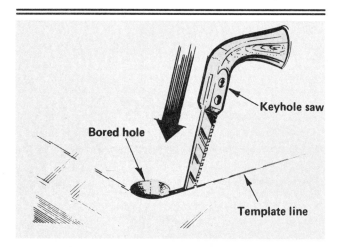

Make cutout with keyhole saw.

Install sink.

sure only on the down stroke and none on the up stroke.

Apply a thick ribbon of caulk around the edge of the cutout where the sink rim will rest, set the sink in place, and press down all around. Wipe away the excess caulk. Follow the manufacturer's directions for fastening the sink to the countertop.

HOW TO INSTALL A LAMINATED HARDWOOD COUNTERTOP

The procedure for installing a laminated hardwood countertop is exactly the same as that for installing a plastic laminated unit, with these three exceptions:

You will need help in handling the material because laminated hardwood countertops are extremely heavy, weighing up to several hundred pounds.

You must exercise greater care with a laminated hardwood countertop because the material can be chipped much more easily than high-pressure plastic laminate.

Corners are butted, not mitred.

HOW TO INSTALL A CORIAN COUNTERTOP

Corian can be worked just like plastic laminate even though it looks just like marble; however, care must be used in cutting this material. It is heavy (so you will need a helper) and will chip or break unless care is taken with it. You should be very careful with this expensive material, for mistakes can cost money. If you lack the time or skill to do it carefully, have the top and cutout made by a professional.

You will need the following tools and materials: A screwdriver, hammer and wedge, level, circular saw (with a carbide blade), router, C-clamps, neoprene adhesive, turnbuckles and screws, scrap lumber, and sandpaper. To install a Corian countertop, follow these steps:

Remove the old countertop and level all the base cabinets. If your kitchen has just a sink front instead of a sink cabinet, you must provide extra support for the new countertop. Corian is very heavy, and it needs support behind the sink. A wooden cleat nailed to the wall can provide support here and at other places—such as the corners—where there may not be adequate support. To provide extra support along the middle, lay a ¼-inch board along the length of the cabinet run.

If you ordered a Corian top with an integral sink, the piece will be cut to the correct depth—that is, 25 inches front to back. But if you ordered a sheet of ¾-inch Corian you will have to cut the Corian to the correct 25-inch depth as well as to the proper length. The best way to cut Corian is to go very slowly with a circular saw equipped with a sharp carbide blade (the blade should be as sharp as possible to avoid chipping). Since cutting will produce a "snowstorm", plan on sizing it outside if possible.

To raise the Corian countertop so that the top surface will be 36 inches off the floor, cut a strip 3 inches wide from the scrap to run the entire length of the top. Turn the Corian over and glue the strip along the bottom front, recessed about ⅛ of an inch, using neoprene adhesive. Be sure you glue so that the factory-finished front edge will face the front. Then do the same along all sides. A ready-made top will already have this done for you.

If you must turn a corner for an L shape, make a butt joint rather than the miter joint you would make with a laminate top. Seal the butt joint with neoprene adhesive. If you wish to draw the two sections of Corian snugger (never tight), you can install a turnbuckle underneath attached to a recessed screw on either side of the joint. Ready-made tops will already have turnbuckles.

You can make a sink cutout in the same manner as in a plastic laminate top, except that a router will do the job faster and better than a keyhole or saber saw. If you use a router, first make a jig of scrap lumber and fasten it down with C-clamps to guide the router. Despite the "snowstorm" of Corian, do not attempt to make the sink cutout outside. The strips at the front and back of the sink cutout would almost certainly break under the strain of supporting the weight of the heavy side portions. Once the cutout has been made, do not move the top without help. Corian fractures easily.

Cutting Corian leaves sharp edges; sand cut edges until they are smooth.

HOW TO INSTALL A CERAMIC TILE COUNTERTOP

Installing ceramic tile is certainly the messiest approach to installing a new kitchen countertop, but it could well prove to be the most durable. You will need the following tools and materials: hammer; keyhole saw; notched trowel; tile cutter or glass cutter and tile nippers (both a tile cutter and tile nippers can be rented where you buy the tile); rubber trowel; and a pencil. A plywood sheet (if a new undersurface is required—¾-inch CDX is best), epoxy or organic adhesive, grout, and a silicone sealer are also required. Follow these directions for simple installation:

Make sure all cabinets are perfectly level; shim at the floor if necessary.

Use a ¾-inch sheet of exterior plywood as the

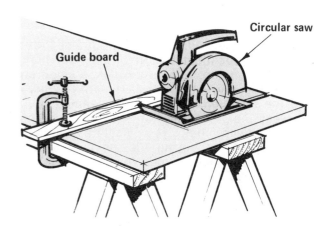

The best way to cut Corian is to go very slowly with a circular saw. The blade should be as sharp as possible to avoid chipping.

base for the tile countertop. Place blocks as necessary under the perimeter of the plywood so that the top surface of the tile will be 36 inches above the floor. If more than one sheet of plywood is required to form the base, leave a ¼-inch gap between the sheets, and fill the gap(s) with epoxy.

Make the sink cutout in the plywood (and any other cutouts such as those for a built-in cooktop or counter inserts), following the same procedure described for a plastic laminate countertop.

You can lay tile "wet," which means in mortar, or you can fasten it down with an epoxy or organic

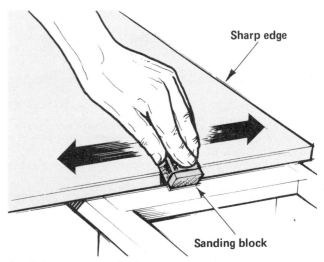

Sand sharp edges on Corian top.

adhesive. The manufacturer of the tile usually recommends a specific brand (or brands) of adhesive. Since the adhesive method is easier and faster, it is the method used here.

Determine the width of the grout line. With sheets of mosaic tile, the width of the grout line is already determined; with larger tiles, a small tab provides the correct spacing. If not, you must make the decision. To minimize cleaning problems, keep the grout lines narrow. The determination of grout width helps you calculate how much tile to buy. When buying tile, be sure to buy bullnose cap or cove pieces for the backsplash and edge pieces for the sink and front edge of the countertop. Buy a few extra because some are certain to break.

Lay the tile out on the counter and plan the grout gaps; then draw the pattern you will follow on the plywood.

Spread the adhesive evenly on the base with a notched trowel. Then lay in the tile, working on just a couple of rows at a time. Put each tile down flat and avoid sliding it; sliding thins the adhesive.

Let the adhesive dry overnight before applying the grout.

Apply the grout with the rubber trowel according to the manufacturer's directions. Hold the trowel at an angle to force the grout down between the tiles. When the grout begins to dry, run the eraser end of a pencil down the grout lines to give them an even depth. Wipe off any excess grout with a damp rag. When the grout is completely dry, spray it with a silicone sealer to prevent oil or dirt from discoloring the grout.

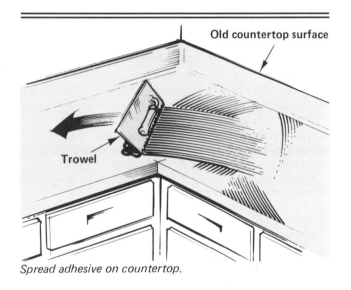
Spread adhesive on countertop.

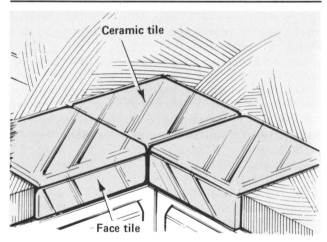
Corner detail on ceramic tile installation.

Set tile on backsplash.

Apply grout with rubber trowel.

Ceilings

Except for application technique, a ceiling can be treated much like a horizontal wall, because many of the same coverings used on walls are also used on ceilings. Paint and wallpaper are the two most common methods of finishing a ceiling. There are, however, several other possibilities including acoustical tile, decorative ceiling beams, and skylights.

Acoustical Tile

The noise levels in the average kitchen can sometimes be very high. Prolonged exposure to such noise levels can be extremely annoying, and can damage the hearing. Acoustical tiles can absorb about 50 to 75 percent of the sound waves striking them. This does not mean they will reduce the noise level by that amount, but they do help considerably. In addition, you get the advantage of a good-looking ceiling that can conceal imperfections.

There are two main methods used to install acoustical tiles. They can be glued or stapled directly onto a solid, level and smooth ceiling in much the same way as laying floor tiles. If the ceiling is badly cracked or marked, furring strips should be installed first; they should be leveled, and then the tiles can be glued or stapled to the strips.

The second method is to suspend the tiles by one of the various systems; this method is especially good if the ceiling must be dropped to hide unsightly wires, ducts or other imperfections. The suspension system can be any form of metal grid hung from wires or attached to the ceiling by nails. The tiles, in turn, rest in metal troughs or tees once the grid is installed. Any of these systems must be leveled properly, otherwise there will be observable dips or high spots.

No matter which of the two systems you choose, look for the following when purchasing ceiling tile:

All ceiling tile is *not* acoustical. It must be labeled with this information; otherwise you may get a nice-looking decorative surface with little sound absorbing qualities.

Ceiling tiles are available in many decorator patterns, with each tile forming part of pattern. However, when installing these tiles, the pattern must be balanced on all four sides of the ceiling; that is, to get a professional look, you must make even cuts on all four sides. An easier alternative is to select acoustical tile with a continuous pattern so that the individual tiles are not detectable.

Ceiling Beams

The addition of ceiling beams offers a nice change from the normal flat ceiling. They are available in either wood or plastic, unfinished or finished. The beams can be cut to fit the width of the ceiling to be covered, and instructions for installation will be included. Plastic beams are especially light and easy to handle, and can be

Material	Do-it-yourself Installation	Durability	Cleanability	Do-it-yourself Repair
Acoustical tile				
Glued or stapled	Easy	Good	Difficult	Fair
Suspended	Fair	Good	Difficult	Easy
Ceiling beams				
Plastic	Easy	Good	Fair	Easy
Wood	Difficult	Good	Difficult	Difficult
Skylights, 2 feet square	Difficult	Fair	Fair	Difficult

bought with realistic carving. Some custom cabinet makers also make beams, and these can be finished to match the cabinet color.

Skylights

Skylights can be a good solution to a daytime lighting problem in a kitchen. Do-it-yourself skylight kits are available, but before you buy one, make sure that you have the room to install it. Check carefully in the attic or crawl space for clearance. Although a light shaft from the roof through the attic and into the kitchen is not very difficult to construct, it is much simpler to install a skylight without one. Also, purchase a skylight made of clear, shatterproof plastic and not glass; this will prevent hail or other weather damage. Look for an insulated skylight—one that has a built-in layer of dead air space.

HOW TO PAINT A CEILING

The easiest way to renew an old ceiling is to re-paint it. Most kitchen ceilings are painted white or off-white because one of the primary decorating principles is to put light colors high and dark colors low. A darker color on a ceiling tends to "lower" it and make the room seem smaller, and usually kitchens are too small already. Very light pastels in the same color family as the walls or countertops can be very pleasing, as long as they are a lighter shade than the walls.

To paint a ceiling, first protect all kitchen equipment with dropcloths. Ceilings should be finished before walls, but if the walls are not to be painted, protect them around the upper perimeter with masking tape.

Using a semi-gloss latex paint, paint around the perimeter of the ceiling with a brush for a distance of about 4 inches. Use a long-handled roller for the wider areas. Go slowly and evenly from one side to the other, always applying new paint against the wet edge. When finished, it is easy to clean up with soap and water.

HOW TO WALLPAPER A CEILING

Applying a wallcovering to a ceiling is backbreaking work and, since you will have to work on a makeshift scaffold, it can be very dangerous. If you plan to do it yourself you will need a vinyl-surfaced wallcovering, paste and other materials. In addition, you will need two ladders and a plank to make a scaffold. Position the scaffold so you can work with your head about 6 or 8 inches below the ceiling. Use the two ladders to support the plank, which must be long enough so you can

work from one side of the room to the other without getting off. You will also need a helper to hold the paper as you apply and smooth it down.

Always hang paper across the room—not lengthwise—because the linear distance is shorter. Snap a chalk line on the ceiling as you would for a wall so you can line up the first strip.

Cut all paper until you have the correct number of strips the correct length to go across the entire ceiling. Allow an inch of overhang at each end of the strips for trimming. If there is a pattern, be sure to index the strips before cutting them so the pattern matches.

If the paper is not prepasted, glue up the first strip, then fold it loosely like an accordion, starting at one end with each fold about 14 to 16 inches wide. Hang the smoothing brush around your neck with a string so it will be handy when you need it.

Get up on the scaffold near the edge where you will start the first strip. Have the helper also get on the scaffold. Unfurl the first few folds of paper while holding it up near the ceiling, and have your helper move the rest of the strip right or left so that you start straight along your chalk line. Smooth the paper on the ceiling with the brush. Check for straightness as you finish applying the strip. Slight unevenness in the corner along the ceiling line will not matter. However, if it is uneven enough to show, apply the first strip so it overhangs the wall by about a half-inch and trim it with a razor knife. Be sure you stay aligned with your chalk line.

Move the scaffold over, and paste and fold the second strip in the same way. Proceed with the other strips until the ceiling is finished.

When you come to a light fixture, turn off the power and remove it. Hold the paper close to the fixture mounting box and slit the paper. Slit the paper outward from a central point; you can trim after the strips around the fixture have been applied. Replace the fixture when finished and turn the power back on. Trim off all excess around walls and sponge down the surface, and the job is finished.

HOW TO INSTALL CEILING TILES

The standard way to install ceiling tile in a kitchen is to nail up 1x3 furring strips on 12-inch centers across the joists. You then staple or nail the tongue-and-groove tiles to the strips. A new method uses metal furring channels; which are self-leveling and concealed beneath the tiles.

This system uses 12x12 inch or 12x48 inch tiles and metal furring channels that are manufactured in 12-foot lengths. These are designed to hold

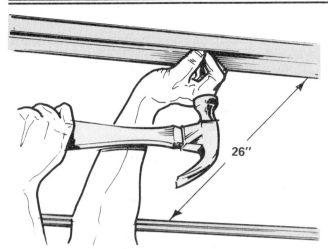

Measure out 26 inches from wall for first furring strip.

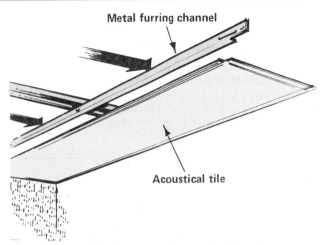

Typical suspended tile system (dropped slightly).

metal cross tees from which the tiles are suspended. To install such a ceiling nail molding to all four walls, 2 inches below the level of the ceiling.

Nail the first metal furring channel to the ceiling, 26 inches out from the wall. A nail is driven every 48 inches along the channel. Remaining channels are spaced 4 feet apart.

Bend the sides of each channel slightly inward and clip on the metal cross tees; the tees slide easily along the channel.

When all channels and tees are in place, start installing tile in a corner of the room; lay the tile on the molding and slide the tee into the concealed slot on the leading edge of tile.

Continue across the room installing full tiles. When a tile must be cut to finish a row, save the remainder and use the leftover piece to start the next row. The tiles hide all supporting members except for the perimeter molding.

Other ceiling tile systems use hanging wires to support the channels and cross tees. This system is excellent for dropping high ceilings, or if you want to include luminous ceiling lighting fixtures.

Locate position of skylight by using nails.

Frame opening between rafters.

These fixtures are engineered to fit with the ceiling system and are the same size as the panels.

OTHER CEILING IDEAS

A skylight can add natural daylight to the kitchen of any one-story house, even when it has a gabled roof. Best of all, it can be installed fairly easily in a day, if the roof is flat.

If the roof is gabled, a "light shaft" can be constructed from the skylight in the roof, through the attic and to an opening in the ceiling of the kitchen. The light shaft can be made of ⅜-inch plywood—just four walls attached on the outside

Apply mastic around edge of hole.

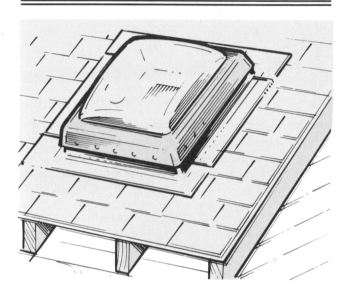

Skylight unit in position after installation.

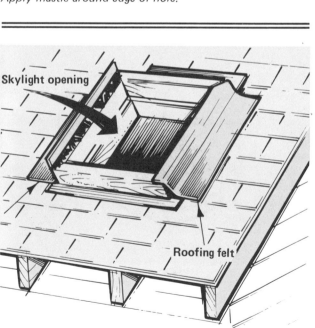

Lap roofing felt over opening (curb mount).

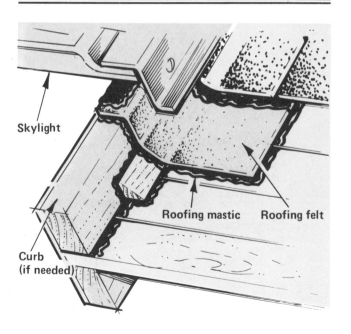

Blowup of typical skylight unit (curb mount).

corners with strapping and screws—and painted white on the inside.

Before proceeding, check the ceiling and the attic to make sure there is a place for a skylight. You may find cooling ducts, wiring or other mechanical elements that cannot be moved out of the way. If the way is clear, buy the skylight to fit between the rafters. These vary in size from 16 to 48 inches square. The roof opening generally will be cut about 3 inches less on both dimensions. Purchase a skylight that is doubled-glazed with a dead air space between, to avoid heat loss in winter or summer cooling problems. Here is how a low-profile skylight is mounted flush to the roof.

In the attic, drive a 3-inch nail up through the roof at each corner for the skylight.

Locate the nails on the roof and remove the roofing material about 12 inches all around the skylight area. Drill holes within the corners and cut the opening for the skylight with a keyhole or saber saw.

Frame the opening at top and bottom between the rafters with the same size stock used for the rafters. Normally these will be 2x6 pine. If the rafters are too far apart to align with the skylight, add framing at the sides. If it was necessary to cut a rafter, tie it into the framing with other 2x6's.

Apply roofing mastic around the entire opening, about ¼-inch thick. Cover all exposed wood surfaces.

Position the skylight over the opening, drill small holes for nails, and nail each corner down into a rafter using 8d nails. Use rustproof roofing nails around the flange itself, spaced about 3 inches apart.

Apply more mastic over the edge of the skylight; but stop short of the cutout and any parts that will be visible from below. Cut strips of roofing felt wide enough to go from the flange to overlap the felt on the roof decking. Put the side pieces on first, then the top piece. Finally, apply a piece at the bottom overlapping the sides to prevent moisture from being trapped.

Apply another coat of mastic over the felt strips and replace the roofing. Apply a bead of mastic across the bottom edges of the skylight.

Ceiling Beams

Ceiling beams can be constructed of ¼-inch plywood or hardboard, miter-jointed where the edges meet and held together with glue blocks inside. Once installed, they can be painted to match the ceiling, or covered with woodgrain self-stick vinyl.

Another easy way to get realistic ceiling beams is to buy them ready-made of polyurethane plastic. These are finished to look exactly like wood, come either smooth or carved. These light-weight beams can be attached to the ceiling with mastic.

Cut the foam beams with a knife or a hand saw. If you want cross beams, they can be lap-jointed where they meet; at this point cut a section out of the bottom half of the beam you put up first and half section out of the top of the beam that crosses it. Measure carefully before making the cuts and make them a half-inch too small. Shave them to fit tightly. This is extra work but the joinery is critical to their appearance, especially on patterned, preformed beams.

You should cut the long beams to fit tightly. To place them, have a helper pull the center of the beam down while you slightly bend the ends into place. Then push the center up.

Hooks and Hanging Implements

Decorative and sturdy hooks are available to hold pots, plants, and other items from the ceiling. Do not use ordinary hardware; instead buy the hooks used for hanging swag lamps. These hooks come in silver, brass, black, and white; screw directly into the joists above your ceiling.

Swag lighting hooks have small base plates, 1 inch or more in diameter that fit tightly against the ceiling. Locate the center of the joist and drive a finishing nail on either side of the spot where you want to place the hook. The nail holes will be concealed by the decorative plate. Use a drill to make a pilot hole for the hook or you may screw the hook in crooked.

Never depend on molly or toggle bolts in ceiling wallboard to support heavy objects. Over a period of time it will slowly pull the wallboard down.

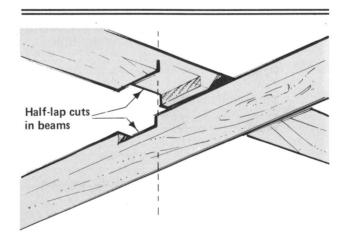

Half-lap cuts in beams

Method of cutting lap joints in ceiling beams.

Walls

Cabinets and appliances cover most of the walls in a kitchen. This would seem to leave little space for anything further. However, there are a lot of things you can do and, with imagination, create something more than areas of white paint.

Kitchen walls can be split into functional or decorative areas. Functional walls are covered with cabinets, windows, or shelves. The wall areas between and above are usually filled with backsplashes and soffits. The rest of the walls can be decorative, complementing and enhancing the total kitchen. If what you put up does not blend well, though, it could negate the whole appearance. Your decorating scheme will probably be with you for some time and if it has a jarring effect, it may make you unhappy with your new kitchen.

Many kitchens open out into other parts of the home. If there is a dining nook or a work area, you should consider the decoration as a whole. A wall that may look great in relationship with kitchen furnishings may not blend with other areas.

Painting

Paint is the most common wall covering. Basic paint types include latex (water-based), alkyd (oil-based), and rubber. The finish can be flat, semi-gloss, or gloss; the latter two are best in a kitchen because they are easier to clean. Latex paints are the easiest to apply and clean. Properly applied, a good paint will last for years and blends with almost any style or furnishing.

When buying latex paint, read the label carefully. Fifty percent or more of the pigment base should be latex solids, and the main pigment ingredient should be titanium dioxide. This gives the paint covering ability. Single-coat coverage paints are more expensive because they use more of both.

Also, if you plan on applying other materials to the walls, choose a neutral color to harmonize with everything. Cool colors recede and should be used for a small room, warm colors do the opposite.

Wall Coverings

So many products are marketed under the name "wallpaper" that it is more accurate to call them all "wall coverings." Common characteristics are that they come in rolls and are applied in individual strips to the walls.

The best product for kitchen use is a material

Material	Do-it-yourself Installation	Durability	Cleanability	Do-it-yourself Repair
Paint	Easy	Good	Very good	Easy
Vinyl wallcovering	Fair	Very good	Good	Fair
Plastic laminate	Difficult	Excellent	Excellent	Difficult
Ceramic tile	Fair	Excellent	Good	Fair
Corian, ¼-inch thick	Difficult	Very good	Excellent	Excellent
Paneling	Easy	Good	Very good	Fair
Real brick veneer	Difficult	Very good	Poor	Fair

with a waterproof vinyl coating. These are usually strippable (you can easily take them down later) and are prepasted. The thicker the material is, the more expensive the wall covering will be. Always purchase one with a vinyl coating because it is so easy to wash.

Consider murals as one alternative. These are large, space-filling designs that come in a kit. You trim the design to match the size of the space you wish to cover. Murals are relatively expensive, but they can produce some unusual decorating effects.

Most murals are not vinyl-coated. If you use one, seal it with a clear silicone finish to protect it.

When selecting a wall covering, consider that they can be difficult to apply. If you do not have time to do the job carefully, have a professional do it for you. Usually the professional will guarantee the job for some time.

You will find it easier to work with a prepasted and strippable wall coverings despite the higher cost. Mistakes can be taken down and put back up again.

Paneling

Paneling is popular, especially in a dining nook. Excellent simulations of brick, stone, wood, and marble are available. Wood veneers are the most expensive. Types vary, but paneling with a vinyl coating is best for easy care. This type is washable, an important consideration in the kitchen. Paneling normally comes in 4 by 8-foot sheets and in a variety of thicknesses. Good paneling is not cheap, but there is no better material to use if the walls are unsightly and have many imperfections.

However, avoid rough or grained surfaces for kitchens, especially in light colors; they tend to collect dirt and can be difficult to clean.

Cheap paneling may look good, but it is unreliable. It is usually on a hardboard base that can chip in installation. It is better to buy quality paneling because it will last longer and has a richer appearance.

Laminates

If you select plastic laminate countertops, consider doing the area between the wall cabinets and the backsplash in a thinner-gauge laminate material that matches. It is best to have this installed professionally. This material is easy to clean and will last as long as the kitchen.

If you decide to do this yourself, check with the fabricator of your countertop; he may have a piece of the same material he used to cover your countertop. If so, he may sell it to you at a reasonable price.

Corian

The ¾-inch-thick Corian material that is used for countertops is available in a ¼-inch thickness for walls. These sheets are 30 inches wide and are sold in up to 10-foot lengths. Corian is quite expensive, but it is easy to clean and extremely durable. Corian may require special bracing and gluing due to its weight.

Ceramic Tile

Ceramic tile can be used on walls in the area between the backsplash and the bottom of the wall cabinets. It is durable, easy to clean, and it is attractive. However, ceramic tile can be highly reflective, especially glazed tile, and the grout can be discolored by stains if not sealed properly.

If you decide to apply ceramic tile to a wall, look for tiling systems that offer tile in prepatterned sheets, some of which are pregrouted. They are easier to work.

Buy enough tile to do the job and a few extras. Some will break in application and if you need to replace a tile later, it may be difficult to find an exact color match.

HOW TO PAINT KITCHEN WALLS

Paints that work well in a kitchen include gloss and semi-gloss latexes, rubber-based paints, or flat and semi-gloss oil-based enamels. The latex paints are easiest to apply and clean up and are quick drying.

When painting walls, you can use a brush or roller. The quickest method is to use a roller, but only after you use a brush to "cut in"; that is, you

Apply a few inches of paint around area you don't want to touch with the roller.

apply a few inches of paint around areas you don't want to touch or mark up with the roller. You should cut in a brush width close to all areas to be left unpainted; after shielding the area with masking tape or a hand-held sheet of cardboard.

When using brush or roller, make sure the walls are clean, smooth and even. Any old, flaking paint must be scraped, and the edges sanded or the new paint will not adhere. Paint the walls after the ceiling. If you are right-handed, start at the left edge or corner and go to the right, working from the top down. A roller requires that you even the coverage by going crosswise after the up and down strokes. Go from one side to the other, from top to bottom, always painting against the wet edge. Try to time it so you can finish in one day. If you start wet paint against a dried edge it will show.

Do not paint too fast with either a brush or roller. Speed causes splatters and makes for unnecessary cleanup problems.

Decorators usually suggest you paint the wood trim the same color as the walls, though you should use an enamel paint on the trim. If you choose to do this, then don't mask off the wood trim. Paint over it with the flat or semi-gloss wall paint, because it makes a good primer coat for the enamel.

HOW TO WALLPAPER KITCHEN WALLS

Most modern wallpapers are not really paper at all. The wall covering often put up in your kitchen—where you have wide variations in heat and humidity—should be a vinyl-covered fabric, burlap, or metallic foil. You can buy these materials prepasted and some are even pretrimmed. It's a good idea, if possible, to buy one that's strippable, because these can be peeled off easily if you want to change later.

A standard roll of wall covering will cover 30 square feet, plus 6 square feet for overlapping, waste, and so on. Rolls come 24 inches wide by 18 feet long or 27 inches wide by 16 feet long. Both cover the same amount. A few of the new metallic foils are 29½ inches wide.

Before choosing the wall covering, measure the area you want to cover and add 20 percent to that figure for wastage. If you have one door and one window in the area to be covered, subtract one roll from the total. For two doors and one or two average-size windows, subtract two rolls. If you want a border trim, this must be measured in feet, because such trim is sold in linear yards.

To prepare a wall that has a prior coating of flat paint, wash it thoroughly, fill all cracks, remove any loose paint, and sand all edges. Then apply a coat of wall sizing, a form of glue that makes wall coverings adhere.

If the wall is covered with gloss or semi-gloss paint, sand it down lightly with medium-grit sandpaper, just enough to remove the gloss. Wash it with an ammonia solution made of one part ammonia mixed with six parts water. Rinse, apply sizing, and proceed.

A textured wall surface must also be sanded reasonably smooth. Then fill any cracks or holes, rinse, and apply sizing. Bare wallboard or unpainted plaster, if smooth and sound, needs only a coat of sizing.

Should there be old wallpaper on the wall, it is best to remove it. Vinyl paper will pull off easily; but often there are one or more layers of old paper. In this case, rent a steamer from a wall covering dealer. Hold the steamer head to the wall and when the paste underneath has softened, use a wallpaper scraper to peel it off. Wash the wall with steel wool and a washing compound to remove any old paste and sizing, rinse thoroughly, and patch any holes. Then apply sizing.

To hang the new wall covering, you will need the following: A chalk line with a plumb bob, paste brush, smoothing brush, seam roller, natural sponge and a trimming knife. You also will need a pasting table. This can be rented, or use a sheet of plywood—ideally about 6 feet long and 3 feet wide—resting on two sawhorses. You can make-do with two card tables placed together, and covered with brown wrapping paper. If you are using a prepasted wall covering, you will need an immersion tray. It is usually made of waxed cardboard or plastic; you can use a bathtub or large kitchen sink.

If you are going to paper entirely around the kitchen, start in the most inconspicuous corner because you will not be able to index or match the pattern at the last seam. This usually is not a problem in a kitchen, because only one or two walls are normally covered.

When hanging wallpaper, you should work from left to right if you are right-handed; right to left if you are not. From the corner along your first wall measure a distance that is one inch less than the width of the roll. Mark the wall. Then tack your chalk line to the wall near the ceiling so it drops through the mark. Hold the weight steady, and snap the line against the wall. This gives you a true vertical line on which to line up the wall covering so it will be straight.

Lay the first sheet of wall covering on the pasting table, and cut it lengthwise to 4 inches longer than your floor-to-ceiling height. Hold it up to the wall to check. There should be about a 2-inch overlap at both the ceiling and floor.

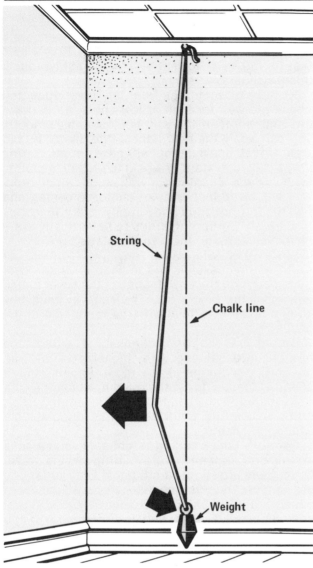

Method of striking chalk line for first strip.

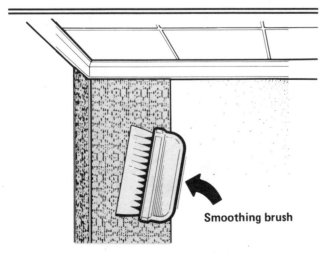

Smooth paper in corners and upper wall.

If it is right, lay it back on the table face up and unroll the covering for the second strip. Make sure that the pattern matches at the left edge of the new strip and the right edge of the first strip. Do not cut until it indexes. Repeat this until you have several strips to hang. Turn the strips over pattern side down.

Mix your paste according to the manufacturer's instructions. Avoid lumps. Tie a string across the top of the paste bucket to hold the brush; this will keep the handle clean.

Apply the paste to the top half of the roll in a figure-eight and then apply paste to the rest of this half, making sure to cover the whole surface. Any unpasted spot will make a blister. Fold the top half over, paste to paste, and apply paste to the bottom half. Fold this half in the same way. This will make it easy to carry the strip to the wall.

At the wall unfold the top half, carefully and accurately position the edge next to the vertical chalk line, and start smoothing the covering toward the corner with your hand. Smooth it well into, and 1 inch around the corner. Then, unfold the bottom half and smooth it the same way.

Use your smoothing brush to work out excess paste and air bubbles, always working toward the edges. Use the ends of the brush's bristles to ease the material tight into the corner along the ceiling and the floor or baseboard. Turn the brush vertically to smooth the paper into the corner. Make sure the material sticks.

Proceed with the next panel, butting it against the edge of the first, and so on, working along the wall.

About 15 minutes later roll the seams with the seam roller. Do not roll hard, but firmly. Rinse each strip after rolling with a natural sponge and clear water; the sponge should be squeezed dry enough so the water will not run. Trim off any excess material at the floor and ceiling with the trimming knife. Have plenty of blades on hand so you can discard the blade after five or six cuts. Blades dull rapidly, and when dull they will easily tear the wall covering.

When you reach a corner, measure from the edge of the last strip to the corner, and add a half-inch. Subtract this total from the width of the roll. Measure this total along the next wall, make a mark, and snap a new chalk line to be sure all strips on the wall will be vertical.

For example, if you have 15 inches from the edge of the last strip to the corner. Add a half-inch. Subtract 15½ inches from the width of your roll (say it's 24 inches) and you have 8½ inches. Measure along the wall a distance of 8½ inches and make your mark for the chalk line.

When you hang the last strip on the first wall

(the sheet that turns the corner), butt its left edge against the right edge of the previous strip. Smooth it and tap it well into the corner. Then trim it vertically a half-inch from the corner on the new wall. Slide the remaining section to the left, into the corner and over the half-inch you already have pasted. Line up the right edge with the new chalk line on the new wall.

Do not try to piece small strips in over windows and doors. Hang a full strip just as though the window or door was not there. Use scissors and cut diagonally from the inside of the door or window and across the corner like a miter joint; this will allow you to paste the paper flat against the wall around the corner. You can trim off excess paper.

To hang a prepasted wall covering, follow the same procedure as described, cutting strips to length and indexing them. To apply a strip, reroll it from bottom to top with the adhesive side out, loosely, and immerse it in the tray of water. Follow directions on immersion time. Then carry the tray to the wall, lift the end of the roll to the ceiling, index it to the line, and place on the wall. Rub and brush out air bubbles.

HOW TO INSTALL WOOD PANELING

Wood paneling is popular for kitchen walls. Relatively easy to apply, especially using the new paneling adhesives, paneling does not require a lot of wall preparation. It can also cover many flaws. The variety of patterns and wood finishes is almost limitless. However, some of the less-expensive panels are not moisture-resistant and for that reason are not suitable for use in the kitchen. It may be better to choose a good plastic-coated paneling instead. Most panel sheets are 4 by 8 feet. Sheets are available in 4 by 10 or 4 by 7 feet for higher or lower ceilings. To apply, follow this procedure:

Remove all moldings from the lower edge and check the wall for high or low spots. Sand down any high spots. If the wall is reasonably smooth, you can apply the new panels directly to the old wall. If it is uneven, you will have to use furring strips (1x2 inch slats of wood) to provide a plumb, level surface. Locate your wall studs, which probably will be 16 inches apart center to center, and nail the furring strips horizontally, every 16 inches to the wall. Cut furring strips to fit vertically every 16 inches and nail them to the studs.

Since this will make any wall outlets or switches inaccessible or too deep for their cover plates; turn off the power, remove the cover plates and reset the boxes out. The edge of each box should be almost flush with the room side of the panel.

Before paneling is installed, it should be brought into balance with the temperature and humidity conditions in the room. Panels should spend at least a day in the room in which they are to be installed stacked flat with full-length furring strips separating them so air can circulate between the sheets.

Carefully check ceiling height at several places around the kitchen before cutting panels to fit. Often there are slight variations. If such variations are no more than ¼ inch you can cut all panels at once. If you are using a circular saw, cut slowly against a guide strip that is C-clamped to the stack because circular saws often tend to wander. Cut panels ½-inch short to allow a ¼-inch gap at

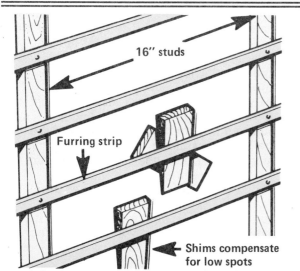

Attach furring strips to level uneven walls.

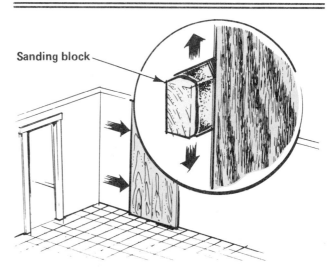

Sand corner panel to conform with uneven wall.

floor and ceiling for expansion.

Stack all panels in position at the wall to check for pattern or woodgrain color. Woodgrains may vary considerably from panel to panel. Place them for the most pleasing combination. Then move them aside and out of the way.

If the first panel will fit into a corner, place it there and check the far edge for plumb. Corners are seldom completely straight, and you may have to sand or file the corner edge of the panel to fit. Do this carefully, because if the first panel is crooked, the entire wall will look uneven.

Apply adhesive to the first panel, going around edges and then in three wavy vertical lines between them from top to bottom. If you are using furring strips, only apply adhesive to the strips.

Press the panel into place, with a ¼-inch gap at top and bottom, and wedge it up from floor with wood shingles. Drive a couple of panel nails at the top to hold it in place. Press firmly all over the face of the panel to spread the adhesive. Now repeat with the second panel, butting it carefully to the first.

Go back to the first panel, put your fingers under it at the floor and pull it out from the wall about 6 inches. Brace it there with a small piece of wood. It will be hinged from the top by the nails you put in. The purpose here is to let the adhesive get tacky. This will take about 10 minutes, during which you can glue and put up the third panel. Then remove the block of wood and press the first panel to the wall, and use a hammer and cloth-covered block of wood to spread adhesive fully and glue panel to wall. Pull out the second panel and brace it and put the fourth panel in place, following this sequence along the wall.

When you come to panels where you will have to cut holes for switches or outlets, measure carefully from ceiling, floor and the edge of the preceding panel. Mark for the cutout on the new panel. Drill pilot holes within each corner of the mark and saw it out with a keyhole saw.

Finish the job off with matching moldings at top and bottom and the outer edges. Where the moldings meet, miter them or use a coping saw to make them fit together.

OTHER WALL TREATMENTS

The conventional wall treatments already covered—painting, paneling, papering with vinyl or plastic laminates—are suited for kitchens because all can be easily cleaned. But there are also artificial brick and stone veneers. These are popular for other rooms of the house. Because they are harder to clean restrict their use to kitchen areas that open to a dining or living area.

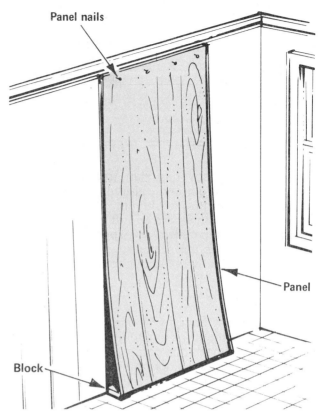

Pull out panel and allow adhesive to become tacky.

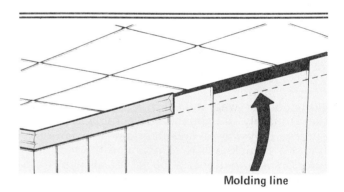

Install moldings to cover uneven panels.

Easily applied with a mastic; they come with directions.

Painted graphics are available in kits. Some just for the wall, others may include the ceiling. If you have a flair for this kind of decorating, you can create your own graphics. If you do, always draw in miniature first so that pattern and colors are pre-established. Outline the pattern on wall, then do it color by color within the masked areas, leaving ample drying time between each color application. Use gloss or semi-gloss paints.

Flooring

The right floor covering can transform a dull kitchen into a bright and colorful one, or a plain kitchen into one that is elegant. Modern kitchen flooring can be either hard or soft, easy to care for or difficult, inexpensive or expensive. Yet the various materials have one thing in common: Nearly all can be installed by the do-it-yourselfer.

Resilient Flooring

By far the most popular choice in kitchen floor covering is resilient tile or sheeting. It is available in hundreds of patterns, colors, and textures, but all types of resilient flooring share several common characteristics. They are all relatively soft underfoot, and need a minimum of care to look their best. Properly installed, any quality resilient flooring will provide years of beauty in your kitchen.

One major consideration in the selection of resilient flooring is wearability. The kitchen is a high traffic area and requires a sturdy floor material. Resilients are available in different gauges up to ¼ inch (thickness of the actual flooring material), with the thicker gauges providing better wearability. Differences in gauge, unfortunately, are almost indetectable to the eye, and the only way to make certain of a particular flooring's thickness is to examine the manufacturer's specifications; price is not always an indication of thickness. Try to buy the thickest resilient flooring available within the limits of your budget.

Quality resilient flooring is also characterized by its ability to withstand indentations. Floors are not only indented by static loads like refrigerators or tables, but also by momentary impact from shoe heels or dropped items. The average person can exert tremendous pressure on a floor, and that pressure per square inch is increased enormously if the person is wearing pointed heels or has a nail protruding from a shoe. Good flooring, therefore, has cushioning to reduce the effects of momentary impact and to provide greater comfort underfoot.

In terms of wearing quality—that is, the ability to withstand the constant abrasion of foot traffic while maintaining their appearance—sheet resilients are better than tiles because there are fewer seams to catch dirt and wear down.

All resilients, even those labelled "no-wax," require regular cleaning, and most no-wax materials need refinishing after several years of foot traffic. Manufacturers recognize this problem and provide a special refinishing solution for use on no-wax floors. The solution does much to restore the original shine of the floor. Some patterns, of course, disguise scuffing and scratches better than others. Textured flooring and complex patterns with dark or multicolored backgrounds look the best. If the kitchen is going to be subjected to an extensive amount of foot traffic (for example, if it serves as a walk-through corridor into another room), you should consider darker or more textured flooring.

Asphalt tile is the least expensive resilient. Usually available in tile form only, this flooring looks good, but it is definitely not as easy to clean as other resilients. In addition, it is brittle; it cannot withstand impact loads very well, and it can break under normal traffic.

Slightly more expensive than asphalt tile and easier to clean, vinyl asbestos tile has a slight cushioning built into it. Thus it provides a softer feel underfoot. It is available in a no-wax version for easy care, and some comes with a self-adhesive backing for easy installation by the do-it-yourselfer. This flooring material is sometimes referred to as "vinyl-composition" tile by manufacturers who shy away from mentioning the hazardous substance asbestos. As used in tile, though, asbestos poses no danger, and it contributes significantly to the flooring's wearability.

Vinyl tile or sheets—generally the most expensive of resilient floorings—come in the brightest colors and the most realistic simulations of natural materials, for example, stone and wood. Vinyls frequently come with "extras" like cushioning and no-wax urethane surfacing, but such extras can drive the price of the material up to almost double that of vinyls lacking these features.

Vinyl resilient is available in rotovinyl and inlaid versions. The pattern on rotovinyls is reproduced by a process much like printing. This process is used extensively for reproduction of natural finishes like parquet or brick, after which the printed pattern is protected by a vinyl coating. Of course, periodic waxing is necessary to maintain the rotovinyl's appearance.

With inlaid vinyl, the design extends completely through the tile or sheet. Inlaid vinyl usually is richer-looking and deeper in pattern and color than rotovinyl, and the design wears better. Regular versions still require waxing to look their best though. While available in tiles, inlaid vinyl is more often sold in sheet goods 6 feet wide or wider. Unless you are handy with tools, it is recommended that sheet goods be laid by a professional because the rolls are difficult to handle.

The no-wax feature involves the application of urethane onto the top of the vinyl flooring, either rotovinyl or inlaid. The surface shines due to a series of tiny ridges, the tops of which wear down while the valleys retain their original luster. The no-wax finish is not permanent, but a dress finish is available to restore the shine that wear has reduced. The dress finish, however, will not last as long as the original finish.

If you plan to install resilient flooring, there are a number of things you should keep in mind.

For maximum wear, see if the flooring you like

Material	Do-it-yourself Installation	Durability	Cleanability	Resilience
Asphalt tile	Easy	Poor	Fair	Fair
Vinyl asbestos tile	Easy	Excellent	Very good	Good
Self-stick	Easy	Excellent	Very good	Good
No-wax	Easy	Excellent	Very good	Excellent
Vinyl tile	Easy	Excellent	Very good	Good
Self-stick	Easy	Excellent	Very good	Good
No-wax	Easy	Excellent	Excellent	Excellent
Vinyl sheet	Difficult	Excellent	Very good	Good
Cushioned	Difficult	Excellent	Very good	Excellent
No-wax	Difficult	Excellent	Excellent	Excellent
Cushioned, no-wax	Difficult	Excellent	Excellent	Excellent
Ceramic tile	Fair	Excellent	Good	Poor
Pavers	Difficult	Excellent	Excellent	Poor
Quarry tile	Difficult	Excellent	Excellent	Poor
Carpeting				
Roll	Fair	Good	Fair	Excellent
Tiles	Easy	Fair	Fair	Excellent
Parquet wood tiles	Good	Good	Fair	Good
Seamless, poured	Difficult	Excellent	Excellent	Poor
Cork tile	Easy	Very good	Good	Excellent

is available in a gauge for "light commercial use." Though the patterns are more limited, flooring made for commercial purposes are thicker and made to withstand heavier impact loads—definite advantages in a heavily traveled area like the kitchen.

Examine the warranty that comes with the flooring, because a defect may only appear after several months or years of use. Read the warranty carefully, and then make sure the flooring is installed according to the manufacturer's instructions. Improper installation can void a warranty.

Cushioning and a no-wax finish are features that boost the price of the flooring without contributing to its wearing quality. If you do not require additional cushioning in your kitchen and do not mind some additional care, such features may not be for you.

If you are not doing your own installation, buy the sheet resilients. The absence of seams will make cleaning easier and reduce the risk of heels getting caught.

Resilients are relatively soft and cannot withstand excessively heavy traffic. If your kitchen is subject to such traffic, you should consider other flooring materials.

Hard Tile Flooring

Ceramic tile and its close relatives like slate, brick, and quarry tile share certain characteristics: They are small pieces of material inlaid in adhesive or mortar to create some kind of decorative design. Grouting material is placed between the individual pieces to finish off the design, and—if done properly—the result is a floor that is durable, colorful, and able to outlast just about any other flooring.

On the other hand, a hard tile floor is expensive, and it can be very hard on feet. In addition, fragile objects dropped on such a floor will almost certainly break. In terms of attractiveness and durability, though, a ceramic or other hard tile floor is difficult to surpass.

Tile is available in two types: glazed or unglazed. The glaze, fused into the tile body during firing, is what gives the hard shine and color to the tile. Also suitable for walls and countertops, glazed tile has a finish that is almost impervious to stains and marks. Unglazed tile has a flatter sheen and is a better choice where reflection could be a problem. When used on the floor, moreover, unglazed tile provides a much firmer gripping surface for walking—provided it is not waxed.

Mosaic ceramic tile, also available glazed or unglazed, differs from regular ceramic in that it is smaller and is mounted on a mesh backing or paper sheet for easier installation. It can also be purchased pregrouted with a waterproof grout/sealant already between the tiles. Pregrouted mosaic sheets make do-it-yourself installation much easier, and the waterproof grout/sealant protects against staining. Of course, having the tiles spaced to the correct distance takes a great deal of the hard work out of the installation. You pay extra for such convenience, but few do-it-yourselfers object to the additional outlay.

Quarry tile is another popular flooring material. Often used outside or in commercial applications, quarry tile is available in either glazed or unglazed types. They commonly come in muted earth colors. The square tiles can range in size from 4 to 9 inches, but curved or geometric pieces are available. They should be installed in wet mortar to ensure a firm bond, and they should only be installed over extremely sound subflooring that can support their extra weight (three or more times heavier than ceramic tile). As a consequence, quarry tile is not recommended for most kitchens.

Slate or brick are just what their names imply: structural materials commonly used for walls that can be laid on a floor. Very heavy, slate or brick is not recommended for use in the average kitchen. If you wish to simulate natural brick or slate flooring, then seek out a ceramic tile or a resilient flooring.

When shopping for any variety of hard tile flooring, be sure to purchase enough so that you will not have to return for more. There will always be some breakage and waste in installation, and tile in any one run will differ slightly in color from another kiln batch. It is better to buy extra pieces than to find that you cannot match the color of the broken pieces.

When choosing a color or pattern in ceramic or other hard tiles, try to be conservative. Tiles are permanent and difficult to cover later if you decide that you do not like them. You can

TILE COUNTER FOR FLOOR TILES OR CARPET SQUARES

Room Area	Number of Tiles Needed (includes waste)	
(square feet)	9x9 tiles	12x12 tiles
40	80	46
80	144	88
100	192	110
150	280	160

eliminate one source of dissatisfaction by making certain to seal the grout. Unsealed grout material will quickly discolor.

If you plan to use hard tile flooring, there are some things to keep in mind.

Unglazed tile is porous and can be stained. Grease will soak into unfired tile, which can make the material a problem in the kitchen; glazed tile, on the other hand, has a slick surface and may cause people to slip and fall. Because of these liabilities, you may want to consider installing such tile *around* the kitchen perimeter and installing a matching resilient in the high traffic areas of the work triangle.

Smaller tiles are easy to lay if they are already attached to a mesh or paper backing. Since the larger quarry tiles should be set in wet mortar, the installation is messy and requires some skill to do correctly. If you are using these tiles in a large area, consider having the work done professionally.

Though it may look good in your kitchen and require a minimum of care, tile is hard on feet. Its reflective surface, moreover, will increase the noise level. Since the kitchen is a noisy place anyway, you may want to avoid adding to the din.

Try not to buy tile that is "on sale" unless you are sure you can get enough to do the job, plus extras. A given run of tile will usually be the same shade, but anything else—even if labeled as being the same color from the same manufacturer—will differ. Such differences are characteristic of the manufacturing process and cannot be helped.

Carpeting

One interesting material for use as a kitchen floor covering is carpeting. An adaptation of the popular material used on patios or in breezeway areas, kitchen carpeting is easy to install by the do-it-yourselfer, looks attractive on the floor, and is extremely easy on the feet. In addition, it absorbs sound. Its wearing characteristics are about the same as the better-quality resilients and it is slightly more expensive than the lower grade of resilient flooring.

On the other hand, carpeting is more difficult to keep clean. Spills are harder to remove from a carpet than from resilient or hard tile flooring. One can quickly lose patience with a material that must be cleaned constantly or one from which stains cannot be removed effectively.

Kitchen carpeting is made of three layers of synthetic material: a nap with a loop or tuft construction, a sponge backing, and a waterproof membrane to prevent any seepage from soaking into the floor. The thicker the construction, the easier on the feet and the more noise-absorbing the carpeting will be.

Kitchen carpeting is available in self-adhesive tiles 12 inches square or in long rolls. The tiles are easy to lay, and any fitting work can be done with a utility knife or scissors. A disadvantage involves the joints between the squares. Spills can seep through the seams to the floor underneath, and the joints may become unsightly.

Rolled carpeting, which can be laid either loosely (with two-sided tape to hold it around the perimeter of the room) or glued down with an adhesive, is better than carpet squares because it has fewer seams. It also permits a nice continuous pattern, and is less expensive than the self-adhesive tiles. Smaller rolls, though, may have to be butt-jointed, and such joints can catch heels or other objects. If the kitchen has many sharp angles, cutting to fit can cause problems.

Make sure that you are getting *kitchen* carpeting and not indoor/outdoor material. The latter is porous and made so that water will soak through and drain away, making it unsuitable for kitchen use. True kitchen carpeting should have a waterproof layer built in to protect the underlying floor.

When deciding between carpet tiles or rolls, remember that tiles are easy to replace should something happen to one or two. You simply remove the damaged tiles and replace them with identical ones. Rolled carpeting requires more effort to repair, and the seam where you make the patch will probably be visible.

Rolled carpeting can be laid with two-sided tape, but it is more permanent when it is laid with an adhesive. This is a messy task at best, and the carpeting is heavy and difficult to handle. If you lack the necessary skills but still wish to install kitchen carpeting yourself, opt for the squares.

Select medium or dark colors. Not only will they not show dirt as readily as light hues, they will also disguise wear. Carpet, in spite of its synthetic nature, is a soft surface and wears.

A busy carpet pattern can clash with the rest of the kitchen furnishings. Therefore, get a sample to take home and match with the rest of the kitchen; you may be surprised to find a pattern that you thought looked wonderful in the showroom does not blend well. Since carpeting covers such a large surface area, it immediately attracts the eye and the careful effect you labored to achieve may be completely undermined by the wrong flooring material.

Wood And Parquet Flooring

Wood is probably the most traditional of all floor coverings. With the proper finish and care, it will last as long as any flooring on the market. Yet that beautiful appearance will last only as long as the material that protects the wood, and that material must be renewed fairly often in a high traffic area like a kitchen. If you are prepared to spend a great deal of time caring for your kitchen floor, wood may be the material for you; you will sacrifice time and work for the beauty that you get.

Regular wood flooring, made of tongue-and-groove strips about 2 inches wide, is normally installed when the home is constructed. This sort of installation requires a great deal of work and is best left to a professional. Traditional parquet flooring—individual strips of wood laid in various patterns—is also a tedious process that requires skill to do properly. In fact, any wood flooring is expensive and difficult to maintain. Therefore, most people opt for a resilient flooring that simulates wood rather than the real thing.

Some manufacturers market parquet flooring that comes in tiles or long planks backed with foam cushioning and coated on the top with vinyl. Some have a self-adhesive backing for installation by the do-it-yourselfer. Actually a cross between traditional wood and the resilients, these hybrid parquet floors offer the beauty of one and the ease of maintenance of the other.

If you decide on wood or parquet, there are some important things to know.

If you are going to have a regular tongue-and-groove wood floor laid, make sure that the installer will guarantee his work. Wood floors expand or contract depending on the moisture conditions, and expansion areas and a solid underlayment are necessary. If the floor starts to warp six months later, you want that installer to stand behind his work.

Wood, like ceramic tile, is hard. Fragile items dropped on it will break, and your feet will tell you that you are not standing on a cushioned surface. Think carefully before having a wood floor installed, because the result is expensive and relatively permanent. You will not be able to change flooring as easily as you can with resilients.

If you must have a wood floor in the kitchen, consider wood tiles with a vinyl or urethane finish. They are not only easier to care for, but they also permit you to replace a damaged area without difficulty.

Special Types Of Flooring

Plywood and particle board can be used as flooring materials, but they are more often used for the subfloor or underlayment. Both can be stained and varnished or sealed and painted. Not as tough and durable as other flooring materials, they require constant care and show wear and stains readily. Therefore, despite their low costs, plywood and particle board cannot be recommended as kitchen flooring materials.

Seamless (or poured) flooring is not widely used in the home, being designed for heavy-traffic commerical application. It is the ultimate in no-wax durability. The actual flooring consists of an epoxy base, some kind of inset pattern or vinyl chips, and a urethane or acrylic top coat. The material will bond to anything, flows readily around obstructions, resists everything except industrial acids, is waterproof, and requires no waxing or buffing. Its chief drawbacks are that it is hard, relatively permanent, and must be installed by a professional for good results.

The nature of cork—a soft and basically spongy material—would make it seem unsuitable for floors. Yet, it offers beauty and a pleasant cushioning effect. Some manufacturers have made cork floors more practical by creating cork floor tiles. These tiles have a self-adhesive backing, come in standard-size squares, and feature a top surface coated with a long-lasting urethane finish. If you like the look of cork, then these tiles—which are available in a variety of colors—may be what you need to do the job while avoiding the inherent shortcomings of the natural material.

HOW TO INSTALL A RESILIENT FLOOR COVERING

Resilient floor covering is nearly always installed with adhesive. Adhesive is especially needed on subfloors subject to seasonal changes in humidity.

Before buying the material, always check the installation instructions. You may find that the resilient flooring you want does not lend itself to easy do-it-yourself installation.

NOTE: The following instructions apply to cushioned, no-wax vinyl sheet, but the steps are quite similar for installing other types of resilient flooring. You will need chalk line, knife, straightedge, trowel, rolling pin or roller, adhesive, and some heavy cardboard.

Read the instructions that come with the flooring completely before proceeding. Then, measure the room as accurately as possible, and diagram the floor plan on graph paper. Note the position of cabinets, closets, doorways, offsets in the walls, and other details. Measure twice to verify your figures.

Take the roll of sheet flooring into another room where it can be spread out. Use the chalk line to transfer the measurements from the graph paper to the flooring, allowing some extra for trimming. Put heavy cardboard underneath the flooring to

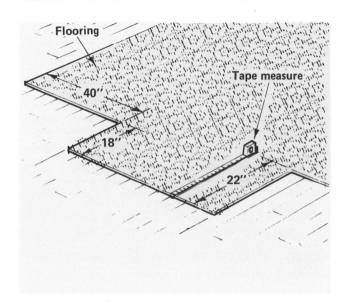

Check measurements carefully.

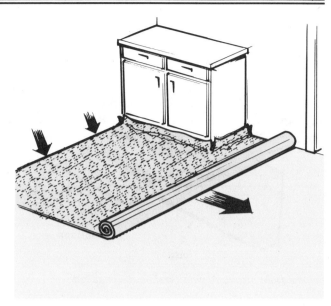

Adjust flooring for fit.

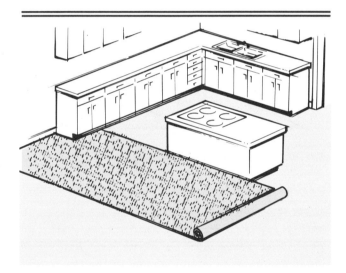

Lay out flooring.

Roll flooring before spreading adhesive.

protect the floor, and cut along the chalk lines with a sharp knife and straightedge.

Carry the flooring back into the kitchen and put it in place; it should fit almost exactly. Trim all overlap with the knife.

Roll back half of the flooring and spread the adhesive on the exposed floor with a trowel. Press the flooring material back onto the adhesive before it dries. Then roll up the other half of the flooring and repeat the procedure.

Finally, roll out the bumps in the material either with a rolling pin or with a special roller available from your flooring dealer. Trim the edges neatly.

HOW TO INSTALL A CERAMIC TILE FLOOR

Installing a ceramic tile floor can be transformed from a very messy and difficult job to one that is relatively simple and clean. You can buy tile with a self-adhesive backing. All you need do is just peel off the protective backing and press the tile in place.

You can lay ceramic tile over gypsum board, exterior grade plywood, tempered hardboard, or almost any other firm base. But never lay tile on a surface that is not perfectly firm or one that has dirt, wax or flaking paint. Always use the proper

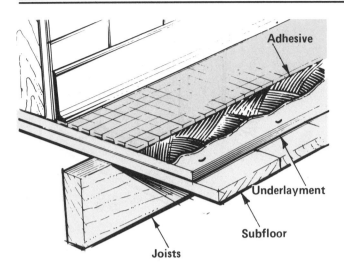

Typical floor structure with ceramic tile installed.

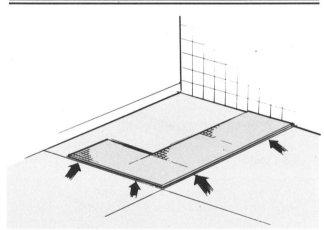

Snap chalk line between opposing walls.

mortar, adhesive, and primer—those recommended by the tile manufacturer—the adhesive *must* be compatible with the surface being covered and with any primer and grout.

If your present kitchen floor is wood, make sure it is sound and firm. Then cover it with ¼-inch exterior grade plywood or underlayment board. Nail down the covering material every 4 inches with ring shank or ring-grooved nails. The nails must be long enough so that more than half the length of the nail penetrates the floor. Long (1¼-inch) staples will work as well and are less tedious to install.

If your present floor is linoleum, cork, rubber, vinyl, vinyl asbestos, or asphalt tile, you can apply the ceramic tile directly to it. But again, make sure the floor is structurally sound, firm, and free of any grease, wax or dirt. The entire surface should be lightly sanded to ensure good adhesion. Badly worn spots should be leveled with underlayment cement. Because ceramic tile is heavy, large areas require a sturdy floor-frame.

To lay tile with pregrouted ceramic mosaic tile sheets, you will need a tape measure, chalk line, notched trowel, tile cutter, tile nippers, utility knife, adhesive, and carpet-covered roller. For caulking around the walls or any plumbing fittings, you will need a tube of sealant and caulking gun. For cleanup, when finished, you will require cheese cloth and high-flash-point mineral spirits. Follow these steps for installing a ceramic tile floor:

Find the center of each of the four kitchen walls, disregarding cabinets, alcoves, and so on. Stretch a chalk line between the centers of two opposing walls, and snap the chalk line onto the

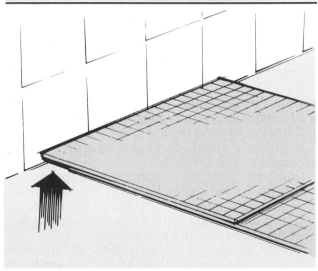

Lay out several sheets of tile.

Check overlap on edges.

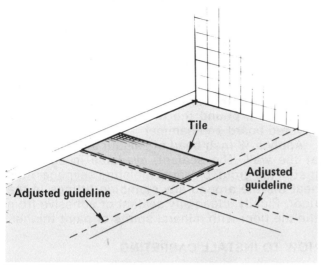

Start at the intersection of the adjusted center lines.

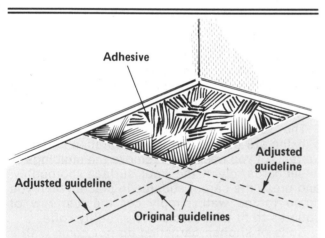

Spread adhesive over space you can finish in 1 hour.

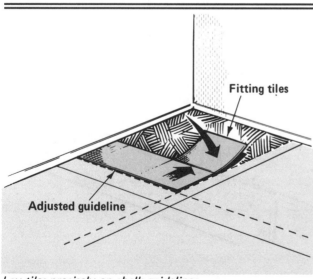

Lay tiles precisely on chalk guidelines.

floor. Do the same between the centers of the two remaining walls. The lines must be perfectly perpendicular to each other.

Starting at the center point of the floor—where the two chalk lines intersect—lay several sheets of tile along one chalk line, and then lay several sheets along the other line—all within the same quarter of the room.

When you approach the wall, overlap the last sheet to see where you must cut the sheet that will butt the wall. If the cut line is in the middle of a tile, move all the sheets back so this cut will fall on a grout line. Do this with the two adjacent walls to minimize tile-cutting. Now, readjust the chalk lines to line up with the sheets of tile. NOTE: If you are laying the tile sheets on a subfloor, adjust the sheets of subflooring so that the seams are at least 3 inches from any joints between the tile sheets.

Starting at the intersection of the adjusted center lines, spread adhesive with the trowel over one quarter of the room—or over that part of it you can finish in one hour or less. If there is an area where you will have to cut the tile—like a far corner—do not spread adhesive there yet.

Lay the first sheet of tile on the adhesive with its two edges precisely meeting the chalk guidelines. Butt each sheet tight against the previously placed sheets, holding the far edge upward so it does not get into the adhesive before the near edges are butted. Put the sheets straight down; never slide the tile into place. Finish laying all full sheets of tile before cutting any sheets.

Cut and fit all sheets that require cutting only at grout lines. Butt the tile sheet against the wall to determine the grout line to be cut, then cut it with a utility knife.

Spread adhesive and lay the cut sheets, pressing them into place between the wall and the other sheets. If your measurement was slightly off and the space is too small, causing the sheet to buckle slightly, take it up and trim along the wall edge with tile nippers.

To determine the cut line for tile sheets that must be cut with a tile cutter, place a sheet of tile precisely on top of the last full sheet of laid tile, and then lay another sheet of tile on top but butted against the wall. Use the edge of the top sheet as a straightedge to draw a line onto the sheet below.

Cut the sheet along the line with a tile cutter. Spread adhesive and lay in the cut sheet, putting the cut edge along the wall.

If you must make contour cuts, such as those around pipes or fixtures, use a soft pencil and draw the shape on the tile as precisely as you can. Cut out all the whole tiles within the line with a

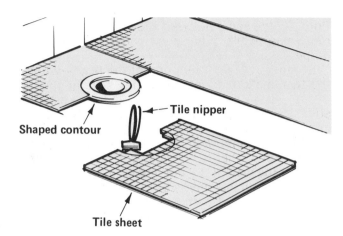

Shaped contour

Tile nipper

Tile sheet

Trim irregular shapes.

Roll out tile floor.

Apply sealant to floor fittings.

utility knife, and use tile nippers to finish cutting tiles within the line.

Wait at least 1 hour after the installation is completed, and roll the entire floor with the carpet-covered roller to make sure that the tile bonds well with the adhesive. In corners where the roller will not fit, pound the tile gently with a carpet-covered board and hammer.

Apply a ⅛-inch bead of sealant along the joint at the wall. The sealant, available in colors to match the grout, prevents moisture seepage. Also seal the tile around any plumbing fittings in the floor. Finally, clean any sealant or adhesive from the tile floor with mineral spirits or paint thinner.

HOW TO INSTALL CARPETING

Carpeting made specifically for kitchens has been around for a number of years. The main disadvantage with any carpeting is that there is no way to get it as clean as the other kitchen flooring materials. On the other hand, kitchen carpeting can be kept adequately clean with ordinary soap or detergent and water, and the impermeable membrane between the nap and sponge backing prevents moisture from reaching the floor.

The 12-inch carpet squares with a self-stick backing are the easiest type of kitchen carpet to install. All you need do is remove the moldings or baseboards, clean the floor surface thoroughly, and press the carpet squares in place. When you come to the wall, simply cut the last row of squares to fit with a scissors or utility knife.

Rolls of kitchen carpeting do not come with a

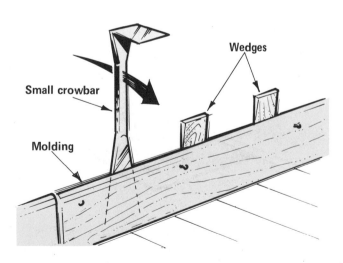

Wedges

Small crowbar

Molding

Remove baseboard and other moldings.

self-stick backing. Instead, two-sided tape (2 inches wide) is applied around the perimeter and—if butting is necessary—additiional two-sided tape (5 inches wide) is applied under the seams.

Follow this general procedure for installing rolls of carpeting: Remove all baseboards and other moldings. Then, lay the carpeting in the room if the kitchen floor is reasonably square. But if the shape of the floor is complicated, make a floorplan. Measure with absolute accuracy, and then carry the carpeting to another room to cut it.

Apply 2-inch two-sided tape around the perimeter of the room, but leave the protective film on the upper side of the tape.

Lay out the carpeting in the kitchen, checking for fit. Now is the time to do any corrective trimming that might be necessary. If you discover spots where you cut the carpet too short, cut small strips from the unused carpet roll to fill in. If the carpet has a pattern, be sure to position patches so that the pattern matches.

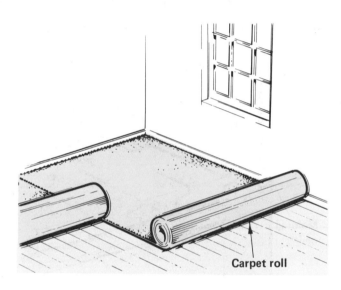

Lay out carpet on kitchen floor.

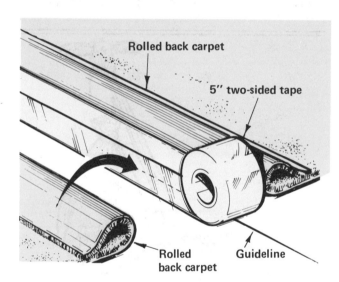

Apply tape for butted joint.

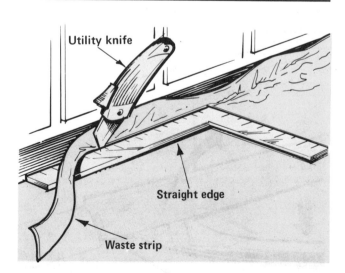

Trim carpet to fit.

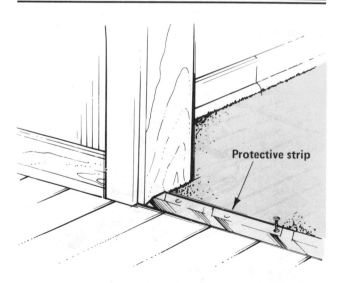

Install protective strip at doorways.

When two pieces of carpet meet to form a butt seam, draw a pencil line on the floor between the two edges, roll them back, and apply 5-inch-wide two-sided tape. The tape should be centered on the pencil line so that each edge of carpet will adhere to 2½ inches of tape. Do not remove the protective film from the top of the tape yet.

Now go around the perimeter of the carpet, stripping off the protective film and pressing down on the carpet. If there are any butt seams, reach under the carpet and pull the film off the tape after the perimeter is secure. Attach any patches.

Finally, replace the molding and baseboards.

HOW TO REFINISH HARDWOOD FLOORS

If you are tired of floor coverings and want to restore the natural warmth and beauty of hardwood, the job is difficult, but it can be done. You will have to remove all vestiges of former finishes and adhesives and strip the floor down to the bare wood. Only then can you apply the new finish.

At a tool rental store rent a drum sander with a dust bag attachment. The store can also furnish sandpaper in various grits. Additional tools you will need include a disk sander, sanding block, hammer and nailset, paintbrush, buffer, and vacuum cleaner. You will also require masking

Sander with dust bag attachment.

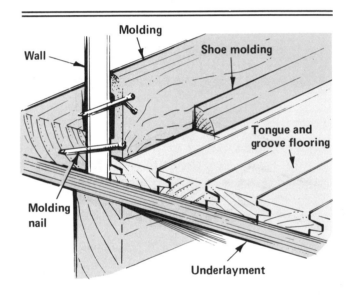

Typical hardwood floor construction.

Floor sanding with hand sander.

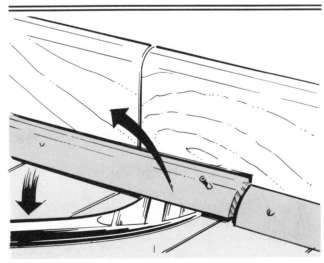

Remove shoe molding.

tape; open coat sandpaper in 20, 40, and 100 grits; turpentine; wax; and the desired floor finish.

To refinish your hardwood floors, follow this procedure.

Move everything out of the room. This includes curtains and draperies, pictures—everything. Floor refinishing is messy, especially during the sanding operation.

Seal off all heating and cooling outlets with the masking tape, and around all doorways except the one you will use (seal that one, too, when you are ready to start). Some sanding dust will get into the rest of the house, but sealing doorways and duct outlets will help reduce the mess.

Carefully remove all quarterround, baseboard and other molding at the floor.

Check the entire floor for nails, and countersink any that protrude. Open the windows.

For the first sanding, use 20-grit paper in the drum sander. Go back and forth over the entire floor, with the grain, overlapping each pass about 3 inches. At the end of each pass, you will have to lift the sander and move it over—but be careful in doing this is avoid digging into the floor. Go slowly.

Use the disk sander or a sanding block in areas near the walls where the drum sander cannot reach.

Repeat the procedure with 40-grit paper, and then again with 100-grit. When you are satisfied that you have removed the old finishes, you can return the rental equipment.

Vacuum the room thoroughly, including the walls and around windows, to remove all the dust. Be sure to remove all dust or you will obtain an inferior finish.

If your floor is pine (frequently the case in an older home), use a special primer to seal the wood. Give the primer an hour to dry before applying your finish.

If your floor is oak, rub some turpentine on a small section to see what the wood will look like with a natural finish. If you like the way the floor looks, you need not stain it. If you decide to stain the wood, apply the stain evenly and let it dry thoroughly according to the directions.

Among the easier clear finishes to apply are the plastic resins, one example of which is polyurethane varnish. The first coat will tack-dry in about 15 minutes, and will be ready for the second coat in about an hour. When the second coat dries, wax and buff. For a high gloss, wait overnight and apply a third coat using a mixture of one part reducer to four parts finish. Let this coat dry overnight before use. After the third coat, the floor will not require waxing and can be shined with a dry mop.

Natural varnish is a traditional finish coat that requires more care to apply. It is slower drying and there is more chance for dust to foul the finish. It is also subject to checking as it grows older, though when applied properly it dries water clear for a beautiful finish. Follow it with a coat of wax and buff.

A NEW WAY TO INSTALL PARQUET FLOORING

A new method for floor refinishing can now give you the richness and elegance of parquet with surprising ease. This new development is a self-adhesive tile made with a hardwood face backed by moisture-proof plastic foam.

These tiles can be laid over any clean, smooth floor. In addition strips are available for doorways that are beveled to the entry floor level. Though not preglued, they can be installed with two-sided tape. You will need a chalk line and a saber saw.

To install this parquet flooring, follow this general procedure:

Remove baseboard moldings, clean the existing floor, and check it for smoothness. Build up any low spots and sand down high spots; if necessary, a new underlayment may be required.

When installing, it is easier to follow the same procedure as in tiling a floor—doing it by quarters from the center. This means that you may need to cut tiles around the perimeter of the room. The fractional pieces will then be the same size on opposite walls; making the job both neat and professional looking.

Peel off the paper backing and lay down, butting them against each other. Make any required cuts with a saber saw. At the walls leave a gap of ⅜-inch for expansion. It will be concealed by the molding. After all the tiles have been installed, replace all moldings.

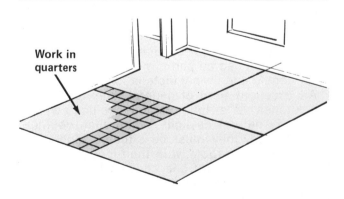

Lay out parquet tiles by quarters from the center of the room.

Electrical Fixtures

Lighting in the kitchen must be planned from two points of view, the decorative and the functional. The decorative aspect is important not so much for the shape of the fixtures, but rather for the way the light affects color. Different types of lighting definitely affect the overall decoration scheme, the appearance of foods, and perhaps even the mood of those who are using the kitchen.

From the functional point of view, you need general illumination for the entire room and localized illumination in the work areas. Such "task" or directional lighting supplements the general lighting and is needed over counter spaces and other work/activity areas in the kitchen.

Artificial light in the kitchen can be either incandescent or fluorescent. Incandescent light is 'warmer'—that is, it is more flattering to skin tones, natural woods and the color of food. The light always comes on immediately, can be hooked to a dimmer switch to control its strength, and the bulbs or fixtures are less expensive than fluorescent tubes. Incandescent bulbs do generate more heat, however, and they consume more electricity to put out less actual light per watt than a comparably sized fluorescent tube.

Fluorescent lighting is more efficient than incandescent, producing about 250 percent more light for the current used. Service life is about seven times that of an incandescent bulb. Cooler in heat output and color rendition, fluorescent tubes provide more even illumination with less glare. There can be a slight flicker or hum, however, this can be partially alleviated with diffuser panels and proper installation.

An excellent form of general illumination for the kitchen is a full luminous ceiling, which simulates natural daylight. When such ceilings are installed, they must be situated along the centerline of the room, with the tubes spaced at least 10 inches apart and covered by diffusers. Keep in mind, however, that luminous ceilings—unless installed in new construction—will drop the height of the ceiling. The distance from the ceiling to the diffuser must be a minimum of 15 inches.

Fixture makers offer what they call false luminous ceilings. These are square or rectangular ceiling boxes with either tubes or bulbs that are surface-mounted on the ceiling. These boxes come in various sizes and can replace the standard single ceiling fixture.

Besides general illumination, you will need task lighting for counter work surfaces and at the sink and range. Counter areas can be well-lighted with undercabinet fluorescent fixtures. Fixtures should be 12 to 18 inches long and spaced about 30 inches apart. Use 15-watt tubes.

When the sink is under a window, you can create enough light for it by using two 40-watt tubes recessed in a soffit and shielded with a diffuser. An alternative would be to use a 75-watt incandescent downlight centered over the sink.

Lighting at the range is usually solved by lights that come installed in the ventilating hood. Typically, such fixtures take a 25-watt incandescent bulb or a 15-watt fluorescent tube; the latter should be the deluxe warm white type for better color rendition. An alternative would be to use recessed lighting or a soffit downlight with a 75-watt incandescent bulb focused down on the range top.

WHAT YOU SHOULD KNOW ABOUT WIRING

If you plan to install lighting yourself—or make other sorts of electrical connections—the first thing you must know is whether you are permitted to do any wiring at all. Most communities have electrical codes, and may specify that all electrical work must be done by a licensed electrician. The first step, therefore, is to get a copy of your electrical code.

In nearly all cases, no matter who does the work, the local authorities will make at least two inspections. One comes when the preliminary work is completed, another when it is finished. When obtaining the code, ask if you will need a permit. Ignorance is no excuse, and you can be subject to fines later if you fail to do something that local law requires.

Before doing any work you should know some

HOW DANGEROUS IS ELECTRICITY?

How much electricity is dangerous? For comparison, normal average household voltage is about 115 or 230 volts, alternating at 60 cycles per second. A standard 100-watt bulb draws a little less than 1 ampere of current, a toaster about 7 amperes. A doorbell operates on about 10-12 volts. In tests, some people were found to stand no more than 7/1000 of 1 ampere at 12 volts AC before having to let go of test leads. Others were able to withstand anywhere from 20 to 40 volts at the same current with leads held in dry hands, but lost voluntary control of arm muscles after only a few seconds. Some with thicker-skinned, calloused dry hands could stand momentary jolts of up to 120 volts, but within seconds the current broke down the skin, caused blisters, and greatly increased conductivity.

Shock sensation occurs at as little as 1/1000 of 1 ampere, and 7 to 8 milliamperes causes severe discomfort. If conditions are right, a current of only 30 milliamperes can be fatal!

When a person receives an electrical shock, two things can happen. One, current interferes with the nerves of the breathing control center at the back of the neck, respiration ceases, and artificial respiration must be started immediately; the nerves may or may not recover. Or, current may stop the heart completely or cause it to fibrillate; the heart may or may not recover. So, take all possible precautions and proceed with care and thought when working with electricity. In the interest of electrical safety, follow these precautions:

1. Before working on any electrical circuit or apparatus, deenergize the circuit by removing plug fuses or tripping a circuit breaker to the "off" position.
2. When deenergizing a circuit, remove a plug fuse entirely and put it in your pocket or toolbox, or securely tape a circuit breaker handle in the "off" position. This will prevent the circuit from being turned back on by someone else. In both cases, post a sign at the main entrance panel telling everyone that electrical work is in progress.
3. Always assume that an electrical outlet or apparatus is energized until you prove otherwise with a circuit tester or by pulling a disconnect plug. Deenergizing the wrong circuit is easy to do, with unhappy results.
4. Do not work on a switched outlet or lighting fixture, even though the switch is turned off, without first deenergizing the circuit. In many switching systems, parts of the circuit are still energized when the switch is off.
5. When working in a main entrance panel, always trip the main circuit breaker to the "off" position or remove the main fuses before removing the panel cover. If possible, cover the top main line connecting lugs, which remain energized, with a piece of corrugated cardboard (a good insulator) wedged into the panel box, to prevent accidental contact.
6. When working in a main entrance panel located over a dirt or concrete surface, or any other surface that might be damp, always lay down a scrap of plywood or plank to stand on to isolate yourself from ground.
7. When working in a load center or subpanel, always deenergize the entire panel by tripping the appropriate circuit breaker in the main entrance panel to the "off" position or by removing the appropriate fuses.
8. Always use tools with insulating handles — wood- or plastic-handled screwdrivers, diagonal cutters with plastic grips, etc.
9. In making electrical repairs or installations, always follow safe, accepted practices, procedures, and techniques, and employ proper, approved materials and devices. Never overload circuits, make open splices or connections, mount inaccessible junction boxes, compromise the integrity of conductor insulation, employ improper materials or equipment, or otherwise occasion a potentially hazardous situation. Ignorance is no excuse; make sure that you know what you are doing and why, when working with electricity. You might not get a second chance.

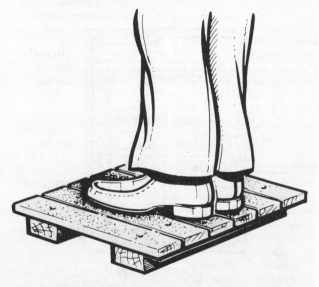

When working in the main panel located over a surface that might be wet or damp, always use a piece of plywood or a wooden platform to isolate yourself from ground.

important things about electricity. The power company supplies electricity through its wires, this passes through a meter in your home and then to a service panel. The power company's responsibility ends at the meter. The service panel is the start of a number of separate, discrete circuits. Each circuit is a small electrical system with a variety of electrical outlets, and each circuit is guarded and controlled by either a circuit-breaker that trips or a fuse that blows in case of overload.

Terms you should know:

A volt is the unit used to measure electrical pressure or current strength.

An ampere (or "amp") is a unit used to measure the rate of flow of electricity or intensity of current draw.

A watt describes current drain relative to voltage. For example, 120 watts at a pressure of 120 volts is one amp (W/V = A). Watts divided by volts equal amperes. Amperes multiplied by volts equal watts (A x V = W).

A typical 15-amp circuit in a home can deliver 1800 watts (A x V = W, or 15 x 120 = 1800). In your kitchen, this could mean a television set that takes 300 watts, a mixing center that takes 400, a toaster that takes 980, and four 30-watt under-cabinet tubes. This adds up to 1800 watts and that should be the maximum for that circuit. Before adding outlets on a circuit, you have to know what the load already is on that line. You can do this only by checking circuit by circuit. Take out the

fuse or trip the circuit breaker to see what doesn't work. You can not assume everything in one room is on the same circuit. One side of the kitchen might be on the same circuit with that side of the upstairs bedroom; another side may share a circuit with a room on the first floor.

The service panel will be found in a metal box near the meter. Called the panel box, it usually has blank spaces for additional circuits. Check to see, since it may be possible to add another circuit.

OVERLOAD PROTECTION

Power is distributed through your house by means of various electrical circuits that originate in the main entrance panel. The 110-120-volt circuits have two conductors—one neutral (white) wire and one "hot" (black) wire. Occasionally, three conductors may be used inside one jacket to serve as two circuits, with one red (hot) wire, one black (hot) wire, and a common neutral or white wire. The 220-240-volt circuits may consist of two hot wires alone, or a third, neutral wire may be added. In all cases, the "hot" lines are attached to fuses or circuit breakers, which, in turn, are attached directly to the "hot" main busses. The neutral wire is always connected to the ground bus, and *never* under any circumstances passes through a fuse or circuit breaker.

Fuses and circuit breakers are safety devices built into your electrical system. Since the typical homeowner probably does not know about wire current-carrying capacity, the fuses or circuit breakers are there to prevent overloading of a particular circuit. Were they not present and you were to operate too many appliances on a single circuit, the cable would get extremely hot, short circuit, and quite possibly start a fire.

To prevent electrical overloads, fuses and circuit breakers are designed to blow or trip, stopping the flow of current to the overloaded cable. For example, a 15-ampere fuse should blow when the current through it exceeds 15 amperes, and a 20-ampere circuit breaker should trip when the current through it exceeds 20 amperes. A fuse that blows or a circuit breaker that trips is not faulty; it is doing its job properly. **Caution:** Never try to defeat this built-in safety system by replacing a fuse with one of a larger current-carrying capacity.

TOOLS

The first requisite is a selection of screwdrivers. These should be good quality tools with insulated handles. You will need at least three sizes for slot-

This is the main entrance panel, main box or entrance box. It distributes electricity to various circuits.

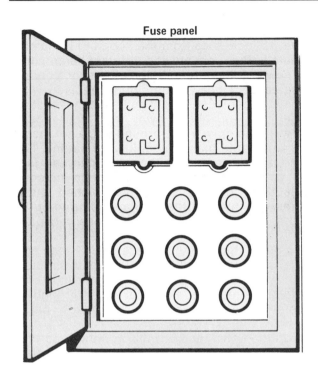

Fuse panel

Circuit breaker panel

In addition to screw-in fuses, a typical fuse panel has a main disconnect and other pull-out blocks with cartridge-type fuses.

Circuit breakers do not blow like fuses; they are switches that automatically trip open to interrupt the flow of electrical current when it overloads the circuit.

ted screws, as well as at least one Phillips-type screwdriver. You will also want a hammer—an ordinary carpenter's claw hammer will do—a pair of slip-joint pliers, and a pair of adjustable water-pump pliers. One or two adjustable wrenches will come in handy. Your electrical toolbox should also contain a tape measure, putty knife, keyhole saw, perhaps a wood chisel, a small torpedo level, either a bitstock or a ⅜-inch electric drill, and a selection of drill bits.

But you will need some specialized tools, too, which you can obtain at any electrical supply house and some hardware stores. Equip yourself with a pair of electrician's diagonal cutters with insulated handles—the kind that has stubby, wide jaws works better than one with long, narrow jaws. An ordinary utility knife is fine for slitting the outer plastic jacket of Type NM or Type UF cable, but for stripping the insulation off the conductors, you should use a wire stripper made for this purpose. Another special tool you will need is a circuit tester to determine whether a circuit is live or dead. Or, you can purchase a more sophisticated—and more expensive—tester that will actually measure voltages and currents.

If you will be working with metal-clad types of

cable, a special armored-cable cutter will save you a lot of time. Installing EMT (electrical metallic tubing) or rigid conduit requires a hacksaw or a pipe cutter, a pipe or tubing bender, and a file and a reamer for deburring cut ends. Conduit work also calls for pipe-threading equipment. If you will be working with modern circuits having three-slot outlets and an equipment grounding loop, a polarity-checking device is very useful. You may need an electrician's snake or fish-wire for fishing cables through walls and ceilings, and a continuity tester for determining whether a dead circuit is open or closed, and for checking ground loops.

HOW TO ADD A RECEPTACLE

Although extending a receptacle circuit is relatively easy, there are a few instances in which it would be unwise to do so. One instance would be when the circuit is already loaded to near capacity. If the circuit is handling only a light load and the new outlet will not add enough to cause an overload, you will have no problem in extending the wiring; but if the circuit is already heavily loaded, do not use it. Instead, run a totally new circuit from your power distribution panel to the new outlet. Do not extend a kitchen circuit, unless to add a clock or to place a receptacle at some out-of-the-way point for convenience only, and where there is little likelihood that an appliance might be used. Instead, run an entirely new circuit. If you can safely extend a receptacle circuit, follow this general procedure:

After you deenergize the circuit, you can start to work on the existing receptacle. Remove the cover plate, loosen the mounting screws, and pull the receptacle out as far as the attached wires permit. Examine the line cable to determine its size; you should use the same size cable for the new outlet. You will probably find it most convenient to use two-conductor nonmetallic sheathed Type NM #12 or #14 gauge cable. If the existing circuit has a bare equipment grounding wire, use Type NM cable with bare ground wire of matching size. If not, either change the entire circuit to a grounded type in the interests of safety and modernization or continue the circuit as an ungrounded one, without the bare conductor, using Type NM wo/g. Under no circumstances should you install a grounding-type three-slot receptacle in an ungrounded circuit—use the old style two-slot receptacle.

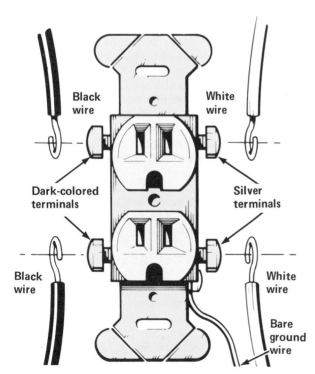

If a circuit is able to handle the additional load, you can add a receptacle by extending the wiring from an existing outlet to the new outlet.

The new receptacle should be at a height of about 12 inches up from the floor, but if the other outlets in the room are at a different height, make the new outlet conform to the others for a uniform appearance. Once you determine precisely where the new receptacle should go, place the electrical outlet box—open end away from you—against the wall and draw a line around it. Do not include any adjustable plaster ears in your outline. Now, turn the box around so that the open end faces you, and refine your outline to include the corner projections on the box. The finished outline represents the area that you are going to cut out of the wall to accommodate the new receptacle box.

To begin the cutting process, drill ⅝-inch holes at the corners of the outline (the holes should be positioned so that their edges will take care of the projections on the electrical box) through the plaster or drywall and into the hollow part of the wall. Insert a keyhole or saber saw into one of the drilled holes, and cut the wall away carefully along the lines that you drew. When you finish cutting, insert the electrical box in the wall to see whether you cut the hole properly. Refine the hole with the saw, if necessary, to provide a suitable fit for the electrical box, but do not attach the box to the wall yet.

At this point, you need to drill a hole in the floor inside the wall, directly below the outlet hole you just cut. Merely locating the right spot can be a tough job. Try measuring carefully, but if that is unsuccessful, remove the baseboard and drive a nail through the floor down to the basement level to give you a point of reference. Be sure, however, that the spot that you select for the nail will be covered after you put the baseboard back in place.

One way or another, you must find that spot for the hole in the between-wall space, directly below the outlet hole. Once you do, drill a ⅝-inch hole up from the basement level. Feed one end of the new cable through the floor hole, into the between-wall space, and up where you can reach it from the hole you made earlier for the electrical box. Pull the cable through the hole and hook it over the edge of the outlet hole so that it will not slip back. Before you can secure the cable in the electrical box, pry out one of the knockout discs. Feed at least 6 inches of cable through the knockout hole and tighten the clamp screw to secure the cable in place.

Push the electrical box—with cable attached—into the wall opening. Fasten the box to the wall stud by driving nails or screws through the holes in the side of the box; or—if you have lath-and-plaster walls—drive screws into the laths through the holes in the adjustable plaster ears. Or install a pair of plaster clips. In any case, make sure that the front edge of the electrical box lines up flush with the surface of the wall.

You can now proceed with the electrical connections at your new outlet. Remove the outer cover from the Type NM cable and strip about ¾ inch insulation from the conductor wires. Attach the conductors to the terminal screws of the new receptacle, and if present, fasten the bare grounding wire first under the grounding terminal and then to the box with a grounding screw or clip. Be sure to loop the conductor wire in a clockwise direction under the heads of the terminal screws. You should also take care to connect the wires so that all the wire without insulation is safely under the screw heads. Clip off any excess uninsulated wire with diagonal cutters. With the wires connected properly, you can fasten the receptacle to the electrical box with the screws provided, and then attach the cover plate to the outlet.

Now, go to the existing outlet and locate a point in the floor inside the wall directly below the outlet. Drill a ⅝-inch hole in the floor from the basement up into the inside wall space; and drill ⅝-inch holes as necessary through the basement joists between the existing outlet and your newly installed receptacle. Your drilled holes should be in a fairly straight path (although they can run at a slight angle), and each one should be at least 2 inches up from the bottom edge of the joist.

Before you can thread the cable through these holes, however, you must do some work on the electrical box at the existing outlet. Remove the box from the wall; remove the screw from the lower cable clamp inside the box; remove the clamp itself; and pry out whichever knockout disc is in the best position to accommodate the new cable. If the 2-by-3-inch box already contains four or more conductors, you must provide a larger one. You can use a so-called "deep box," a box extension or you can gang another box to the original if it is of the gangable type.

Thread the free end of the Type NM cable through the joist holes from the new receptacle to the hole you drilled below the existing outlet. Then comes a tricky assignment; you must feed the cable up through the hole in the floor and pass it through the opening in the wall. If you have trouble, try running a stiff wire through the floor hole up into the wall. Once you get the stiff wire in place, you can pull it out of the opening. Then tape the wire to the end of the Type NM cable down in the basement, and use the wire to help pull the cable up through the opening in the wall.

Once you have enough cable so that you can make the electrical connections, secure it so that it cannot slip back. Go back down to the basement and examine the cable run through the joists. If there are any points where you had to change the direction of the cable run from going through the joists to passing alongside a joist, make sure that you did not put any sharp right-angle bends in the cable that could weaken the copper conductors and damage the insulation. The way to change direction in a run is to put a generous loop in the cable. If you do run cable alongside a joist, fasten a staple not more than 12 inches from the hole where the cable emerges, and then at least every 4½ feet along the run.

With the cable linked to both the new outlet box and the existing receptacle location, go to the existing receptacle and prepare the new Type NM cable for its electrical connections. Slip the cable into the box, along with the existing cables if you had to remove them to get the box out, tighten the cable clamps and slip the box back into the wall. Remove the outer cable cover; bare the wire ends; and attach white wire to silver terminal, black wire to dark-colored terminal. If they are present, pigtail the new and existing cables' ground wires to the receptacle grounding screw and to the box with a grounding clip or screw. Reconnect the other line wires to their proper terminals.

Caution: Make all connections under terminal screws, but never try to attach two conductors under the same screw head—it is considered an unsafe electrical procedure. You will find two screws on each side of the receptacle; they are provided just for what you are doing; extending wiring without making any splices. If you have three black wires and three white wires, connect one of each to appropriate receptacle terminal screws. Join, or "pigtail," each of the two remaining pairs with wirenuts to short lengths of scrap wire, and connect the pigtail ends of the scrap wire to the appropriate receptacle terminal screws that remain. Pigtail ground wires to the receptacle grounding screw and to the box.

When you finish attaching wires to the terminal screws, put the existing receptacle back into its box and fasten it down with the same screws that you removed earlier. Attach the cover plate, restore the circuit's fuse or trip the circuit breaker, and test your new receptacle with a table lamp.

NEW LIGHTING FIXTURES

It is a relatively simple task to hang a new lighting fixture in the same electrical box that served a previous fixture, but it is a bit more complicated when you want to add fixtures to a ceiling or wall that previously had no fixtures whatsoever. Nonetheless, you can handle these installations yourself but the job does require some advance planning. Naturally, work is much simpler when you can install the fixture before the plaster or the drywall is up. You can put a new fixture in a finished kitchen, but in such cases you must cut into the walls to install the wiring and electrical boxes.

You may already know exactly where you want to locate the new lighting fixture and the new wall switch. Switch location is more a matter of practicality than aesthetics. Most people, when entering a darkened room, reach to their right to find the light switch. Therefore, your new switch should be to the right of the entry and about 4½ feet above the floor. If possible, install the electrical box that holds the switch alongside a wall stud; the stud provides a secure point of attachment. You can, however, install the switch elsewhere if you use the kind of box that has a flare clamp to hold it against wallboard or if you secure a standard box with a pair of plaster clips.

In describing the installation procedures for a

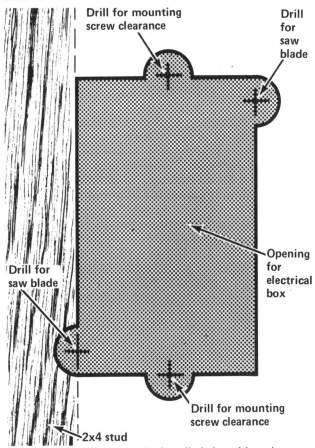

Electrical wall boxes may be installed alongside or between wall studs. If you plan to install a box next to a stud, this actual-size template can be used for some types of standard electrical boxes.

new lighting fixture, we will assume that you want the light fixture in the ceiling of the kitchen and that you will use Type NM nonmetallic sheathed cable for the project. The new wiring will go through the attic (to the ceiling fixture), the basement (to the main entrance panel), and the walls. Therefore, buy enough Type NM cable—the kind that contains two #12 or #14 insulated conductors and one bare conductor (the conductor size is stamped on the cable)—to run from the main entrance panel to the fixture and switch, with a 6- to 8-inch length of cable inside each electrical box. Since you will do everything else before you connect the cable to the electrical system, you need not disconnect any circuits until you reach the final procedures.

Place an electrical switch box—open end facing the plaster or drywall—at the wall location that you selected for the switch. Draw a pencil line around the box as you hold it against the wall; but be sure, as you draw the outline, not to include the plaster ears of the electrical box. Then turn the box so that the open end faces you, and refine your outline to include the corner projections on the box. Follow the same procedure to outline a 4-inch octagonal box on the ceiling at the fixture location.

The outlined areas must now be cut out of the wall and ceiling. Drill ⅜-inch holes through the plaster or drywall at the corners of your outline into the hollow part of the wall. Drill the holes so that the edges will take care of the corner projections on the electrical box. Now, starting at the drilled holes, cut away the plaster or drywall along the lines of your outline, using a keyhole or saber saw. Cut out the electrical box areas for the wall switch and for as many ceiling fixtures as you plan to install.

Next, mount the box for the ceiling fixture (do not mount the wall switch box until later). You will need a hanger bracket to mount the ceiling box, and you can choose whatever type of bracket works best.

Carefully measure below the floor and above the ceiling to determine the points directly below and above the wall switch. While you are in the attic, drill a ⅝-inch hole through the floor so that you enter the wall cavity at a point directly above the wall switch; and, while you are in the basement, drill a ⅝-inch hole through the ceiling so that you enter the wall cavity at a point directly below the wall switch. Drop a string weighted with a nut or bolt from the attic floor hole, and retrieve the string at the large hole you cut earlier for the wall switch electrical box.

Once you get to this point, you need someone else to help you for the next few steps. The other

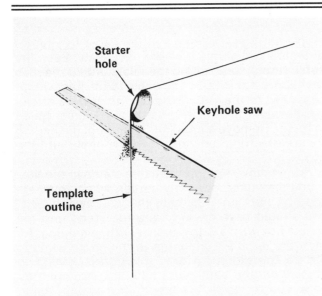

After drilling holes in the wall for an electrical box, the blade of a keyhole saw or saber saw can be inserted to cut the opening.

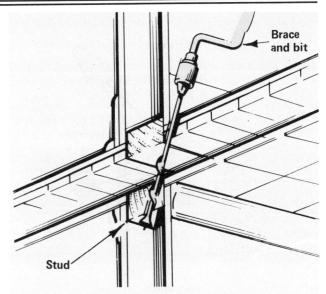

To route cable between the switch box and the ceiling fixture, drill a hole through the attic floor to enter the wall cavity directly above the wall switch opening.

person should go up to the attic. Remove the weight from the string and attach Type NM cable to the string at the wall switch hole. Bare the conductor ends of the cable, bend them in a loop, tie the string to the loop, and cover the joint with tape to make it smooth enough to go through the hole in the attic floor without snagging.

Feed the string and cable up into the hollow wall space through the wall switch hole as your assistant pulls them up through the hole in the attic floor. The string is a big help in getting the cable up through the wall space, but you and your helper must be careful. Do not rely primarily on the string; instead, push the cable to feed it up to the attic. Pulling hard on the string is a sure way to separate it from the cable. Have your assistant pull through enough cable to reach the ceiling fixture box, with an additional 6 to 8 inches for installing the cable inside it. Once the cable passes through the hole in the attic floor, of course, your helper can remove the string and work with the cable itself.

From your position at the switch box hole, cut the cable where it enters the wall, but allow 6 to 8 inches extra for the wall switch electrical box that you will install later. Then have your assistant push a stiff wire up from the basement through the ceiling hole to where you can reach it through the switch box hole. You can then use the wire to pull the cable upward. Once your helper attaches the Type NM cable to the wire in the basement, pull it toward the switch box hole. But again, you should not rely so much on pulling the wire as on

someone pushing the cable up from below. Feed the cable up the wall and out through the switch hole about 6 to 8 inches. Have your assistant take the other end of the cable to the main panel. There should be 6 to 8 inches extra on the cable length to allow for connections at the main panel.

With the cable in position at the switch box hole—one end leading up to the fixture box in the attic floor and the other end going down to the main panel in the basement—you are ready to install the cable in the electrical boxes. Remove one knockout disc from each end of the switch box, feed in the two cable ends, and fasten the cables with the clamps in the switch box. Push the box into the hole you cut earlier, and fasten it to the wall stud with nails or screws through the holes in the side of the box; make sure, however, that the front edge of the box is flush with the surface of the wall before you fasten it. If your walls are lath and plaster or wood instead of drywall, you can use the plaster ears to attach the box to the wall.

Now come the all-important electrical connections; be sure to follow directions carefully. Slit the outer cover of each cable end inside the electrical box, peel the cover back, and cut it off. Then, remove the last inch of insulation from the ends of the black and white wires. The best way to remove the insulation without nicking the conductors is to use a wire stripper; be sure to select the right cutting slots in the stripper jaws for the size of conductors.

Twist the white wires from each cable together firmly and attach a wirenut to cover the joint.

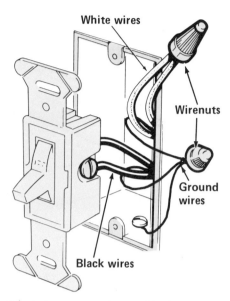

At the wall switch, connect the two black wires to the switch, and join the two white wires with a wirenut. Twist one end of a length of scrap copper wire together with the ends of the two bare ground wires and join them with a wirenut. Secure the other end of the scrap wire to the switch box with a grounding clip or screws.

Twist the two bare wires and the end of a length of scrap bare copper wire together and attach a wirenut. Secure the other end of the scrap bare copper wire to the switch box with a grounding clip or screw. Loop one black wire under each of the two screws on the switch, and tighten the screws. Be sure to loop the wires in a clockwise direction under the heads of the terminal screws so that as the screw heads are tightened they draw the wire loops in tighter. You should also take care to connect the wires so that all the wire without insulation is safely under the screw heads. Clip off any excess uninsulated wire with diagonal cutters. Switching is always done in the black or "hot" wire, never in the white (or neutral) wire; therefore, the black wires and not the white ones go to the screws on the switch. When you complete all the electrical connections, mount the wall switch in the electrical box and attach the cover plate.

Go to the attic and drill holes through the joists in a line from where the cable enters the attic floor to the joist nearest the ceiling fixture. The holes should be in the center of each joist to keep the cable down far enough to prevent anything from hitting it. Feed the cable through the drilled holes. If you come to a point where the cable runs alongside the joist instead of through it, make a loop—not a sharp bend—in the cable to alter its direction and staple it where necessary. Feed the cable through and along the joists until it reaches the fixture box. Staple the cable to the joist within 12 inches of the end of the run; no staples are required when the cable runs through holes drilled in joists. Remove a knockout disc from the ceiling fixture electrical box and feed the cable into the box.

From below, tighten the cable clamp in the box. If you measured correctly earlier, when you were passing the cable up from the wall switch hole, you should have enough wire to extend into the fixture box with a 6- to 8-inch length remaining. Attach the lamp fixture wires to the cable wires in the ceiling electrical box, joining black wire to black wire and white wire to white wire, and the bare wire to the fixture box. Cover all wire joints with solderless connectors, and hang the fixture according to both the type of hardware and the instructions that the manufacturer provides.

Now, go to the basement and drill holes through the joists in a line to the joist nearest the main panel box. Feed the cable through the drilled holes and staple it along the joists until it reaches the main entrance panel.

Up to this point, you have not needed to concern yourself about the dangers of live current, but now you must be careful. **Caution:** Turn off the main circuit breaker—or pull the main fuses—to disconnect all the circuits in your home from the incoming power lines. You will need an auxiliary light source now because all the circuits in your home are dead. That is not to say, however, that you have eliminated any possibility of receiving a dangerous shock. The wires at the top of the main panel box are still energized. Remove the cover from the box, but be very careful to avoid those power lines at the top.

With the cover off, tap a tapered punch against the side of a knockout disc to start its removal; then finish the job with pliers to break the disc out of the box wall. Naturally, the knockout disc you choose to remove should be the one most conveniently located to where your cable run ends. Fasten a cable clamp in the hole, pass the cable through, and tighten the clamp.

Look for a spare circuit in the box. Correlate the wire conductor size to the circuit breaker or fuse rating: #12 to either a 15- or a 20-ampere rating, #14 only to a 15-ampere rating. Strip off the outer cable cover, remove about ½ inch of insulation from each of the conductors, and slide the straight bare end of the black wire under the terminal screw (not under the screw head) that is alongside the circuit you selected. Fasten the white wire and the bare ground wire in the same

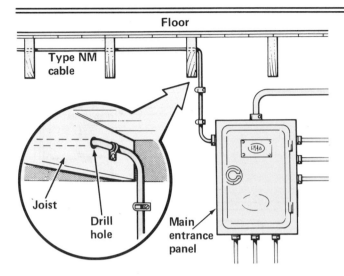

The cable must also run to the main entrance panel. Again, it may run through joists. Where cable runs alongside a joist instead of through it, staple ot clamp it as necessary.

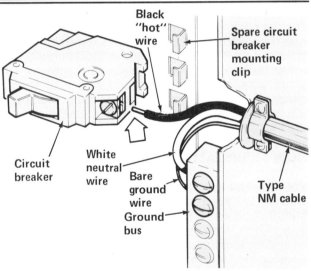

To connect the cable to the circuit breaker, strip off the outer cable cover, remove about 1/2 inch of insulation from each of the conductors, and slide the straight bare end of the black wire under the terminal screw--not the screw head--alongside the circuit breaker. Fasten the white wire and the bare ground wire under separate available terminal screws on the ground bus.

way under separate available terminal screws on the ground bus.

Once you place the cover back on the main panel box, trip the main circuit breaker back on or restore the main fuses, and place light bulbs or fluorescent tubes in the new lighting fixture.

The switched fixture wiring arrangement just discussed is called a "switch-feed system,"

because the power to operate the light comes directly from the main panel to the switch, the "hot" line passes through the switch and the neutral passes by, and both continue to the lighting fixture. Thus, the switch is actually inserted directly in the "hot" side of the power line to the light. A variation on this is to connect that power line to some source other than the main entrance panel, a situation that often is more convenient and makes for easier wiring than running all the way back to the main panel (such a line, incidentally, is called a "home run"). You might, for instance, be able to handily run your power feed line from a nearby junction box, a duplex receptacle or even another lighting fixture box. To do this, though, there are conditions to be met, other than ready access.

First, there must be a "hot" wire and a neutral available in the outlet that you choose, a condition not always true of fixture or even junction boxes. Second, the power source in the box must be, of course, 110-120 volts. Third, the circuit of which the box is a part must be lightly enough loaded to accept the additional load of the fixtures that you are installing without causing an overload or a marginal loading. And finally, the addition of two more conductors must not crowd that electrical box beyond the limits established by the National Electrical Code (NEC). These limitations, as well as formulae for calculating box conductor fill, can be found in the NEC. However, if a box is already full, you can usually get around the problem by ganging on another box or adding a box extension.

There is also another method of wiring a switched fixture, called the "fixture-feed system." Here, instead of the power line going through the switch to the fixture, it is routed directly to the fixture outlet box from the nearest appropriate source. A separate switch loop is run from the fixture to the switch. The system goes together by running one cable from a power source to the fixture box. Run another cable from the fixture box to the switch box. Connect the black wire to one side of the switch and the bare equipment-grounding conductor to the switch box with a grounding screw or clip. With an indelible felt-tip pen, paint the white conductor black, and attach it to the other switch terminal. At the fixture box, connect the black line wire to the black switch-loop wire with a solderless connector, and attach the bare equipment-grounding conductors to the fixture box. Connect the white line wire to the white fixture wire with a solderless connector. Color the white switch-loop wire black, and connect it to the black fixture wire. Other parts of the lighting fixture installation are done in the same way as previously explained.

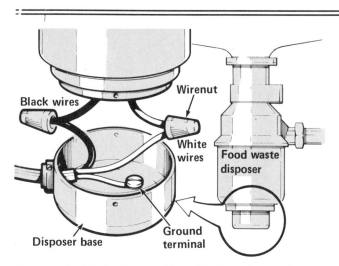

Connect the black wire in cable to black appliance wire, white wire in cable to white appliance wire, and a bare ground wire to a special grounding terminal or available screw that provides a suitable ground.

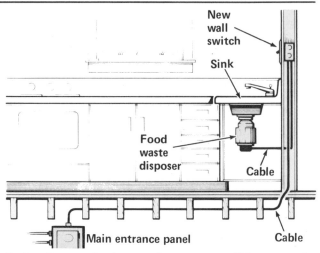

To install a new food waste disposer, you will have to make an opening in the wall for a switch near the disposer and for the cable run to the disposer, and be able to run the cable for the new branch circuit to the main entrance panel.

HOW TO INSTALL A DISPOSER

If you plan to install a new food waste disposer, you must make sure that there is a spare branch circuit in your main entrance panel. If no spare circuit is available for the new built-in appliance, you will have to install a 20-ampere circuit breaker. Obtain enough cable (Type NM #12-2 with ground or other type as necessary) for a run from the appliance to a wall switch, and from the switch all the way back to the main fuse box or circuit breaker panel.

You will need to make openings in the wall for a switch near the disposer and for the cable run to the disposer. Plan the installation so that both holes are between the same two wall studs. From the basement or attic space—whichever is more accessible in your home—drill a third hole in a location that allows you to feed the cable into the wall (again between the same two studs as the switch opening). Fish the cable into the inside wall space and out through the hole for the switch. Then, feed the cable through and alongside the joists and back to the main panel by the most convenient route.

Run another length of cable through the wall from the switch opening out through the hole near the disposer. At the location where you will install a single-pole toggle switch, run both cable ends into a switch box, tighten the cable clamps, and mount the box in the wall—preferably to a wall stud, but otherwise with plaster clips. Follow the procedure outlined in the section "New Lighting Fixtures" describing how to install a new switch box and switch.

Mount the disposer to the sink according to the manufacturer's instructions. With the disposer's

bottom cover removed, connect the cable from the new disposer switch to the disposer and replace the bottom cover. Ordinarily, the electrical connections are as follows: black wire to black wire, white wire to white wire, and bare or ground wire to a special grounding terminal or, in lieu of that, under any available screw that provides a suitable ground to the metal of the disposer.

HOW TO INSTALL A DISHWASHER

You will find that the installation of a built-in dishwasher involves much the same kind of wiring as the built-in food waste disposer, except that there is no wall switch. With the dishwasher away from its final mounting location, drill a hole in the wall or in the floor space, and run a length of cable (Type NM #12-2, with ground, or other as required) back to the main entrance panel. Attach the cable to an existing or newly installed 20-ampere circuit breaker or a fuse socket. **Caution:** If you connect the new dishwasher to an existing circuit, make sure that a current overload does not result.

Move the dishwasher into place, and attach the cable to the dishwasher wiring following the diagram attached inside the appliance. With the dishwasher timer turned to "off," put in the fuse or turn on the circuit breaker to energize the circuit. That completes the installation, and you can now try the dishwasher. It is not necessary to run the appliance through its entire cycle, however. Simply advance the control knob to the various positions, leaving the knob in each position only long enough to verify that each function—rinse, wash, dry—operates properly.

Plumbing

Most localities have plumbing codes that govern what can or cannot be done. Before doing anything, obtain a copy of your community's code and find out if you require a permit. You may discover a licensed plumber is necessary. Also, disposers may be mandatory or they may be prohibited.

To put it simply, plumbing is putting pipes together so they will not leak. Though it takes skill to plumb out an entire house, the do-it-yourselfer can handle smaller projects and do a job that will stand up to normal use. However, before attempting even smaller jobs, you should be familiar with general plumbing work. Plumbing can be complicated in older homes, so unless you are sure you know what you are doing, it may be safer to have the work done by a licensed plumber.

PLASTIC PIPE

Over the years, many types of pipe have been used to conduct water; common in most homes are galvanized steel, copper or, the greatest boon for the do-it-yourselfer, plastic pipe. There is one handicap to using plastic pipe—many building codes prohibit some or all uses of it. However, these codes are likely to change in the future because plastic pipe possesses so many fine features. It is difficult to say which one of the many aspects of plastic pipe is its most advantageous. It is not subject to corrosion, scaling or rust; it is virtually self-cleaning; it will not rot, and usually it does not sweat; it can withstand freezing temperatures much better than metal pipe can; and it is so light that plastic pipe is easier to

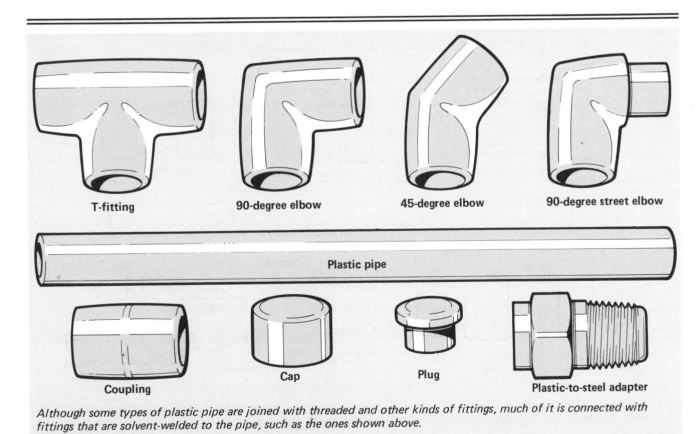

| T-fitting | 90-degree elbow | 45-degree elbow | 90-degree street elbow |

Plastic pipe

| Coupling | Cap | Plug | Plastic-to-steel adapter |

Although some types of plastic pipe are joined with threaded and other kinds of fittings, much of it is connected with fittings that are solvent-welded to the pipe, such as the ones shown above.

handle than just about any other kind of pipe. In addition, because plastic is a more flexible substance than metal, plastic supply lines virtually eliminate water hammer and the need for installing air chambers; it damps vibrations and does not carry sound well. Plastic pipe has low resistance to water flow and consequent excellent flow rates; it is the easiest to install.

There are several types of plastic pipe in common use today for various home plumbing applications. CPVC (chlorinated polyvinyl chloride) pipe is rigid and used for hot and cold water distribution systems. PB (polybutylene) pipe is a new, highly flexible tubing used for the same purpose as CPVC pipe, as well as for water supply lines; PB is especially easy to route into difficult-to-reach areas.

Plastic pipe can be joined—where local codes permit—to other types of pipe by special adapter fittings. For example, if your existing plumbing is galvanized steel pipe, you can make the connection easily with an adapter designed specifically for linking plastic to galvanized steel pipes.

COPPER PIPE

One type of pipe that is on the approved list in nearly every local plumbing code is rigid copper pipe. Relatively lightweight and easy to handle, copper pipe is one of the most popular types of pipe in use. It resists corrosion and scaling; in fact, it is so durable that under normal conditions the copper pipe that you have today will probably outlast both you and your house. Moreover, the smooth inside surface of copper pipe offers little resistance to water, a property that allows a copper pipe of smaller diameter to handle the same job performed by larger pipes made of some other metals.

Flexible copper tubing can do just about anything that rigid copper pipe can do, and plenty more besides. You can bend the tubing around corners or snake it through walls and over ceilings more easily than you can maneuver rigid copper pipe. However, installations made with flexible copper tubing are not as neat as those made with rigid copper pipe. So, flexible tubing usually is used where it will be concealed from view. Its biggest advantage, though, is in the fact that it comes in rolls of up to 100 feet or more. When you work with rigid copper pipe, you usually must sweat-solder sections to be joined, and every connection is a potential source for a leak. With flexible copper tubing, however, you just unroll the length you need; the only connections you have to make are at each end of the run.

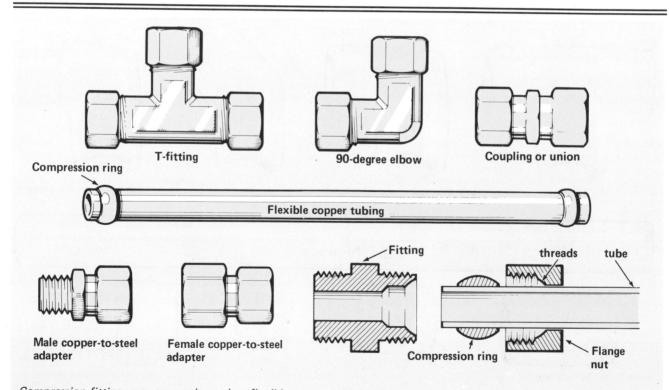

Compression fittings are commonly used on flexible copper tubing. Their use, however, is more expensive than sweat-soldering the tubing; but they can be taken apart easily with open-end wrenches.

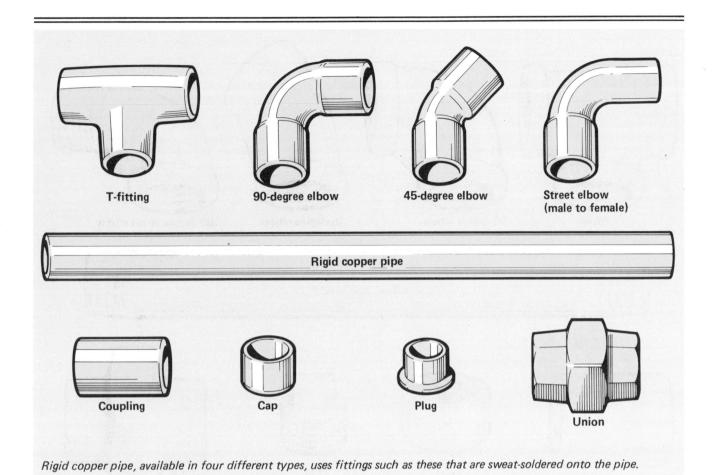

T-fitting **90-degree elbow** **45-degree elbow** **Street elbow (male to female)**

Rigid copper pipe

Coupling **Cap** **Plug** **Union**

Rigid copper pipe, available in four different types, uses fittings such as these that are sweat-soldered onto the pipe.

Fewer joints, of course, mean fewer chances for a leak and allow a better water flow.

Cutting copper pipe or tubing without kinking it takes care. So avoid sawing copper, if possible; use a tubing cutter instead.

Copper pipes or tubes can be joined in several ways. Sweat-soldering is the most common and least expensive way of joining copper pipe, while flare fittings and compression fittings are used mainly for flexible tubing.

GALVANIZED STEEL PIPE

Although copper pipe and tubing have replaced galvanized steel pipe as the most popular type for new home water supply lines, galvanized pipe—which used to hold a monopoly on the supply pipe market—still offers some distinct advantages. For example, suppose your pipes run through a garage or basement or any other area where they are exposed to blows from cars or tools. For such situations, you would be much smarter to use galvanized steel pipe because it is very tough and much better able to withstand damaging shocks.

The price you pay for using galvanized steel

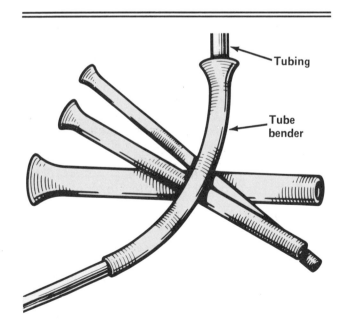

Tubing

Tube bender

To make sharp bends in flexible copper tubing without kinking it, you can use a tube-bender, a spring-like tool that is designed for this purpose.

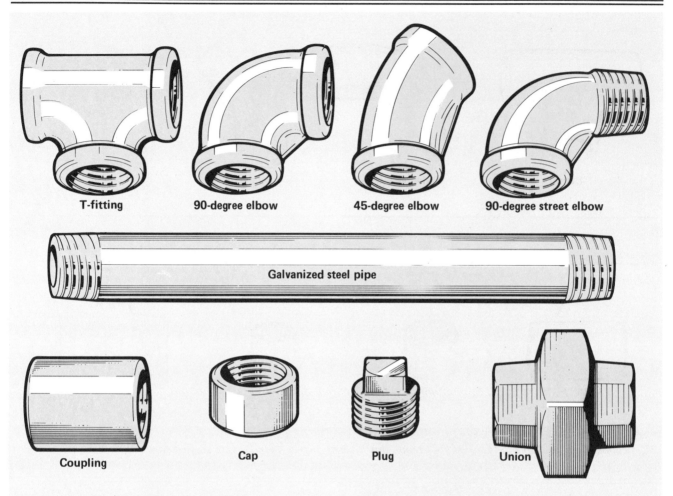

| T-fitting | 90-degree elbow | 45-degree elbow | 90-degree street elbow |

Galvanized steel pipe

| Coupling | Cap | Plug | Union |

Galvanized steel pipe is joined with threaded fittings like those shown here. Such pipe, however, takes longer to cut, thread, and join than copper pipe or tubing.

pipe is both an advantage and a disadvantage. On one hand, galvanized pipe is much less expensive than copper at the time of initial purchase. On the other hand, galvanized pipe is much more expensive to repair. It takes so much longer to cut, thread, and join galvanized pipe than it does for copper pipe or tubing that labor costs will be very high if you have to call in a professional plumber.

PIPE TOOLS

Many plumbing tools, of course, can be used for other do-it-yourself tasks around the house; but no matter how much or how little you plan to use a particular tool, it should be the best of its type that you can afford. Often a good tool will last a lifetime, whereas a poor tool may not make it through the project for which you bought it.

Although the tools you decide to purchase depend on how deeply you are involved in home repairs in general and in plumbing projects in particular, there are certain basic tools that any self-respecting do-it-yourself plumber should have in his toolbox. For working with galvanized steel pipes, you will need pipe wrenches. These wrenches are generally used in pairs; one holds like a vise while the other turns a fitting or a pipe. A strap wrench can be used on polished or plastic pipe without damaging them.

Copper pipe and copper tubing require some special tools. Since you should avoid using a hacksaw on copper pipe, be sure to have a tubing cutter in your toolbox. A small-size cutter, moreover, makes it much easier to work in close quarters, and you will be amazed at how many plumbing chores are performed in cramped surroundings. You will also need a propane torch for sweat-soldering and a flaring tool for making flare connections at pipe joints.

Just like copper pipes, galvanized steel pipes

also require some special tools. When cutting such pipe, you should have a combination vise—one that has a section with pipe jaws—or a yoke or a chain vise, both of which are made especially for pipe work. A pipe cutter tool is easier to use than a hacksaw, but be sure that the cutter is designed for galvanized steel pipes; the tubing cutter for copper is very similar in appearance. Of course, you must be prepared to remove the burrs created by cutting. Outside burrs can be removed with a file, but you will need a reamer to remove any burrs inside the pipe.

Although you can generally purchase the galvanized steel pipe you need already threaded, you may wish to do your own threading. If so, you will need special dies that come in sizes for threading all standard pipe diameters. Whenever you are cutting or threading pipe you should use a cutting oil.

Very few tools—none of them special—are needed for working with plastic pipe. Rigid plastic pipe can be cut with a fine-toothed hacksaw (or, if you prefer, a plastic-tubing cutter); flexible types can be cut with a sharp knife. On most common types of plastic pipe, fittings are joined with solvent cement. On other types, usually compression or threaded fittings are used; they are simply tightened with an adjustable open-end wrench.

TRAPS AND SHUTOFF VALVES

Before doing any plumbing work, you will have to find the main water shutoff, which is normally located near the water meter where the water enters the house. Once the main water shutoff is closed, open all valves in the cold water lines to drain them. Hot water should be shut off where it leaves the water heater, then drain those lines. Otherwise, you may destroy your water heater. Once drained, the lines will not drip when you disconnect any pipe. This will also allow you to sweat-solder if you are working with rigid copper pipe or tubing.

Most plumbing fixtures are installed after everything else in the immediate area has been completed. This is because some fixtures are intended to rest on finish coverings. With others, later installation is simply easier and reduces risk of fixture damage. The specifics of fixture installations are quite variable. But the fixtures usually come with detailed instructions for easy installation. In general, making the connections involves installing traps as necessary between the fixture drain outlets and the fixture drainpipes, and attaching the water supply lines to faucet assemblies. Shutoff valves should be installed in water supply lines at all fixtures.

Directly beneath the drain outlet of your kitchen sink is the trap. This element is vital not only to the proper functioning of the drainage system, but to your health and safety as well. The trap is designed to maintain a "plug" of water within its curved section to prevent harmful sewer gases from entering.

Trap assemblies and parts to fit just about any possible installation requirement are readily available. Chrome-plated thin-wall brass traps are popular. Polypropylene (PP) plastic traps feature ruggedness and longevity, and will outperform all other types. ABS plastic traps are also in use, but are susceptible to deformation and eventual failure when handling frequent passage of boiling water and caustic household chemicals. And, they may not be allowed by your local plumbing code.

Any do-it-yourselfer who installs a fixture without also installing a shutoff, or supply stop valve, is only doing a partial job. You will discover the truth of this statement—if you have not already—the next time a plumbing crisis occurs and you must waste precious time running to the main water shutoff valve.

Fortunately, you can add shutoffs to your plumbing fixtures at relatively modest cost. Whether you work on a sink or an appliance, the shutoff principle is the same. You must remove a section of water supply pipe that runs to the fixture from the floor or the wall, attach the shutoff valve to the remaining piece of pipe sticking out of the floor or wall (called the stub-out), and then connect the shutoff to the fixture with a flexible pipe, usually a chrome-plated copper tube.

The kind of stub-out pipe you have dictates the kind of fittings that you will need. A threaded pipe

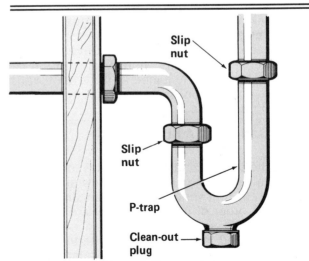

The typical sink (P) trap is illustrated above.

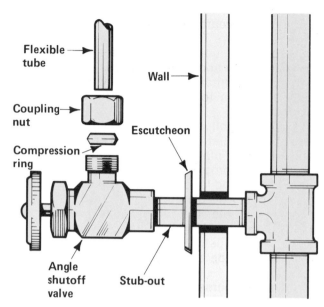

The shutoff valve is connected to the stub-out. A flexible water supply tube runs from the valve to the faucet.

naturally requires a threaded shutoff; a copper stub-out takes an adapter that you must sweat-solder at one end, but which is threaded at the other end to accept a threaded shutoff valve. For flexible copper tubing and some plastic pipe, mechanical adapters can be obtained. Rigid plastic pipe, however, requires a plastic adapter that is screwed to the shutoff valve and solvent-welded to the plastic stub-out. If the stub-out comes from the wall and the fixture is located above it, for example, you need an angled stop valve to turn the water flow at a right angle. However, if the stub-out for that fixture comes from the floor, you use a straight stop valve.

The flexible chrome-plated copper tube, or connector, makes installing the final connections easy, because it saves you from cutting or piecing pipe together to join the shutoff valve to the fixture. The connector is joined to the shutoff valve by a flare connection, compression fitting or compression ring fitting.

HOW TO INSTALL A KITCHEN SINK

One of the easiest and quickest ways to give your kitchen a new look is to put in a new sink. There are basically four varieties of kitchen sinks on the market. In order of popularity, they are stainless steel, pressed steel, cast iron, and an integral bowl(s) molded into a Corian countertop. If your dealer has a large inventory, he may also have the cultured marble or the vitreous china types. Both

are uncommon and because of maintenance problems they are not recommended for use in the kitchen.

The stainless steel sink that you see in the showroom is not really "stain"-less. All will show marks, and the durability of the finish depends on the composition of the steel. Stainless steel sinks will have a percentage of chrome added to preserve the finish and a nickel content that helps to withstand corrosion. You will want to get the largest percentage of each you can find. Cheaper models of stainless steel sinks are constructed of 20-gauge stainless, while more-expensive ones are 18-gauge. The heavier ones will take more punishment and are less noisy during use.

Cast iron and pressed steel, which may be called enameled ware, enameled steel, or porcelain-on-steel, have a surface material that is baked on after the sink shape is made. Porcelain will chip, but you can buy porcelain sinks in a wide variety of colors. Cast-iron and pressed-steel sinks are easy to care for and will last a long time if you do not use an abrasive on them.

Corian sinks are molded directly into the countertop. The price is high and that is a reason why they have not been installed in many kitchens. They are, however, available in either single- or double-bowl models. Corian will scratch and nick, and while such marks can be sanded out, they do require more care than other types.

You can purchase any of these sinks in a variety of shapes and sizes. The standard size is one that is 22 inches deep (front to rear), 33 inches wide (in a double bowl), and 7½ inches in depth. Variations are available, as are corner models to fit in the countertops used in L- or U-shaped kitchens.

On the back of all sinks is the deck or a mounting platform with three or four openings. These are for the faucet-and-spout assembly with its incoming hot and cold lines, a sprayer, and other appliances. If you choose to install an instant-hot-water device and there is no room, an extra hole can be cut into the deck. Integral drainboards are another optional feature with any type of sink. When purchasing a sink consider the following:

Be sure any sink you buy is coated with a sound-deadener, especially if you plan on installing a disposer. A sink can act as a sounding board and create many unwanted echoes.

If you want stainless steel, buy the heaviest gauge sink you can afford. The literature should say 18-8 (the respective percentage of chrome and nickel) or series 302 or 304 (industry designations). A satin or brushed chrome finish is the easiest to care for.

Finally, cast-iron sinks are heavy so there is less noise from water splashing. These sinks, however, can chip, and while they can be touched up, it will show. Check the length of the warranty period. In addition, the finish on porcelain is a coating that will wear well if it is not abraded—you should not use abrasives on porcelain sinks. Sinks come in two types—those with a separate steel rim or those that are self-rimming. Both are connected to the countertop with clamps provided with the sink; you must follow the specific instructions that come with the sink. All types require that a sealant be placed under the rim to provide a watertight seal between the countertop and the sink edge. New sinks come with specific installation instructions, so use the following procedure as a general guide:

If you are installing the new sink in an old countertop, first turn off water supply and remove the old sink. In a new countertop, cut out the opening, using the template provided, or have it done wherever the top is made. Be careful to go slowly and use a router or saber saw. There will be a slight clearance for the sink to fit in, but it is not much. Try the rim after the cutout is made to make sure.

Install the faucet-and-spout assembly on the sink. It is secured by large locknuts on the threaded stems of the hot and cold water faucets. Make sure the rubber gasket is in place around the rim of the assembly, so water will not leak under the sink.

Place a ⅛-inch bead of plumber's putty around the underside rim of the strainer body, and set it in the drain opening. Attach the metal and rubber washers over the screw threads, followed by the large locknut. Slide on the strainer sieve, tighten the next locknut, and insert the tailpiece that connects the strainer body with the drainpipe. Tighten all the nuts with a large pipe wrench, but be careful that you do not tighten them so hard as to chip the porcelain on the sink.

Apply a ¼-inch-thick bead of plumber's putty around the rim of the countertop opening. If using an old countertop, make sure all old putty has been removed.

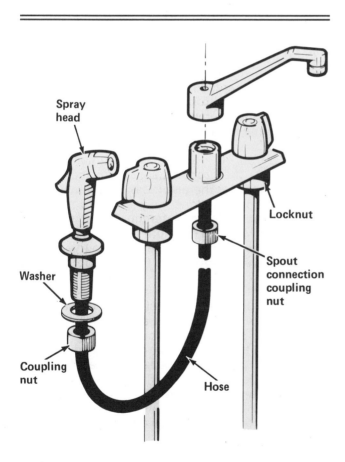

The actual faucet and, perhaps, spray head are the last fixtures to be installed.

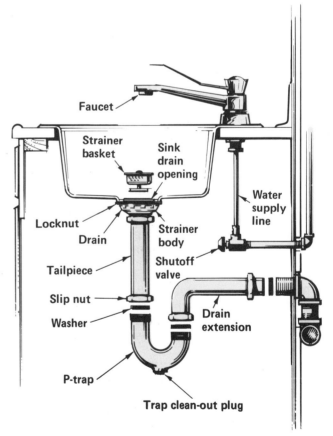

Blowup of a typical kitchen sink installation, showing traps, fittings and pipe.

Lift up the sink and put it into the countertop opening. Slide the clips into the grooves or channels underneath. If the sink requires fasteners to be located on the counter rim, do this before dropping in the sink (the installation instructions will specify this). Tighten the fasteners firmly, but not tightly; overtightened fasteners may crimp or bow the sink top. Check for a tight fit between sink and countertop on all sides before proceeding.

There should be shutoff valves on the water supply pipes coming from the wall; if not, now is the time to install them.

Galvanized steel pipe requires tightening of the unions and pipe sections after liberal application of pipe joint compound. Work from the wall pipe union to the faucet stems.

Copper pipe requires that all joints be sweat-soldered. Compression fittings have to be tightened securely, but be careful not to overtighten them because the metal is soft and can twist out of shape.

Finally, install a P-trap from the tailpiece of the strainer body to the drainpipe. Tighten all sections of the assembly securely, then turn on the water supply and check for leaks.

HOW TO INSTALL A DISPOSER

A disposer sounds like a rather dull and mundane product, but it can be an important aid in kitchen cleanup. An in-the-sink food waste disposer will help you keep your kitchen free of odors caused by wet garbage.

Better units can handle virtually any type of waste—soft foods, stringy foods, rinds, and even corncobs. Unlike many other products, better disposers are quite different from inexpensive bargain units. Quality units have stainless steel grind/impeller assemblies, sink flanges and drain housings. They also have heavy-duty motors. Inexpensive units may not stand up well to tough food wastes. Overloading and jamming can be the troublesome result of a unit not built to handle a tough job.

There is also the matter of safety. Heavy-duty models usually have an anti-jam system of some type. Such systems reverse the grinding direction or use some other mechanism to clear obstructions.

Sound insulation is another primary difference between inexpensive units and quality disposers.

Disposers come in batch-feed and continuous-feed models. Both have advantages, as well as specific modes of operation.

Batch-feed units are slightly more expensive to purchase, because the "wiring" is already done on these models. They have the on-off switch control in the cover. Thus, they are slightly less expensive to have installed. You load it, put in the cover, and turn it to the "on" position to activate the unit. You cannot add additional wastes without stopping the unit.

Continuous-feed units are wired through a wall switch. These units require an additional cost to install. However, the units are less expensive to buy. With a continuous-feed model, load, put in a cover that prevents garbage from flying out yet allows water into the unit, and turn on the wall switch. Additional wastes can be added while the unit is running, although this is not recommended. With the safety cover removed, items can fly out or fall into an operating disposer.

Consumers replacing a disposer probably should stick to the existing type to keep installation simple.

In general, any home with a standard kitchen sink will accommodate a disposer. However, if you have a septic system, check with a local expert before installing a unit.

Disposers are equipped with a sink flange to fit the disposer to the sink at the drain and with full instructions on how to install the unit. Models vary, but the procedure here is typical.

First, check the code to find out if the unit is permitted in your area and if you are permitted to install it. If you are, get the necessary permit. This installation calls for plumbing and electrical work. **Caution:** Whenever you propose to tackle an appliance maintenance task, repair, or new installation, be sure that you first disconnect the appliance from its power source. Either pull the plug, remove the proper fuse, or trip the correct circuit breaker for the electrical circuit involved.

Read the instructions fully and examine the unit's components to determine what you will have to buy. Make all measurements, and note the position of hot and cold water lines to the faucet. You may have to move them to make room for the disposer.

If your unit is a continuous-feed disposer, you will have to buy a switch and switch box and the wiring to connect it. If it is a batch-feed model, you will not need a switch; the top of the unit serves this function when closed and turned. Disposers should have a separate 15-amp circuit. Even if you do the plumbing installation yourself, you may want to call an electrician to put a special circuit with a wall outlet under the sink.

NOTE: If you plan to add a dishwasher at some other time remember the dishwasher needs a separate 20-amp circuit. Have the electrician install both at the same time.

The procedure will be to install the sink flange assembly to the sink drain and then mount the

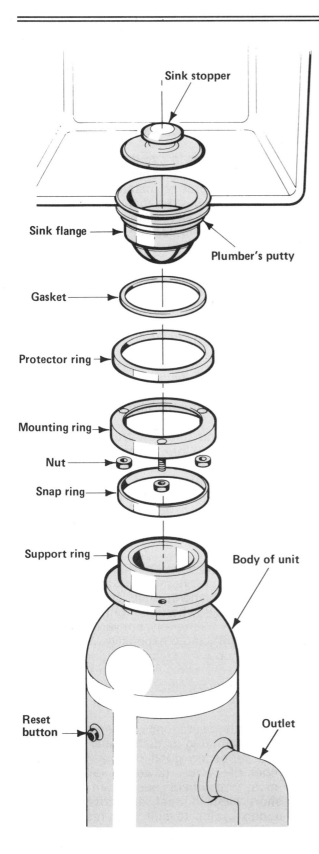

Sink stopper

Sink flange

Plumber's putty

Gasket

Protector ring

Mounting ring

Nut

Snap ring

Support ring

Body of unit

Reset button

Outlet

Garbage disposer showing standard fittings and installation location.

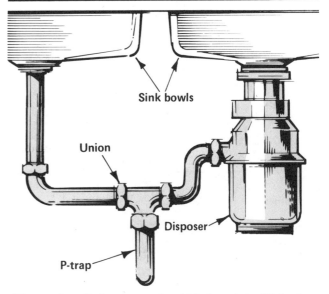

Sink bowls

Union

Disposer

P-trap

Disposer installation on two-bowl kitchen sink. While there are many sink varities, basic installation technique is the same for almost all types.

disposer to the flange. Then cut the pipe pieces to fit, make the plumbing connections and, finally, the electrical connections. Study the position of everything first to determine accessibility. With many models, it is necessary to make all electrical connections first.

The disposer also has a plug that can take a drain line from a dishwasher. If you plan a dishwasher now (or later), this drain plug will have to face the dishwasher.

Begin by removing the sink's tailpiece and trap with a wrench. Also remove the sink drain flange, as well as any sealing material or gaskets. Clean the area around the drain opening in the sink. Now, place a ring of plumber's putty around the underside of the new sink flange, and insert the flange into the drain opening in the sink. Press—do *not* rotate—the flange in place. Remove any excess putty from around the flange. Once you set the flange, do not try to turn it.

From below the sink, slip the gasket over the underside of the sink flange, followed by the protector ring with the flat side up. The mounting ring—with three threaded pins screwed into it—follows the protector ring. While holding these parts in place above the groove on the flange, push the snap ring up along the flange, until it snaps into the groove. **Caution:** If you spread the snap ring, it can become too loose to hold in place around the groove. You may find it slow going to push the snap ring in place, but it *will* go. Make sure it fits firmly in the groove.

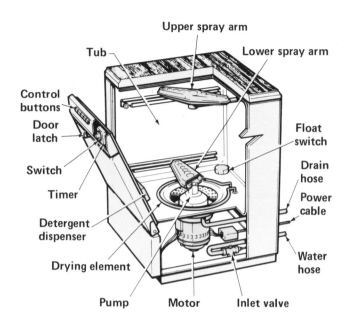

Upper spray arm

Tub

Lower spray arm

Control buttons

Door latch

Float switch

Switch

Drain hose

Timer

Power cable

Detergent dispenser

Drying element

Water hose

Pump   Motor   Inlet valve

Typical dishwasher.

The threaded pins have slots for a screwdriver; they must be uniformly tightened against the protector ring to hold it and the gasket snugly against the bottom of the flange. Tighten the slotted pins evenly, keeping the mounting ring level and tight.

Now, lift the disposer and put it in place. Match the holes in the top of the disposer with the threaded pins, but before tightening the nuts that hold the disposer in place, make sure that its outlet pipe faces in the right direction for its connection to the drainpipe outlet. Tighten the nuts.

Now you are ready to hook up the trap to the disposer's outlet pipe. Use a P-trap if the drain goes into the wall or an S-trap if it goes down into the floor. Do not allow the upsweep of the trap to get as high as the outlet from the disposer. The P-trap entry into the wall also must be slightly lower than the drain from the disposer or it will malfunction or backup. Use the slip nuts and washers; remember that the parts of the trap—the tailpiece, trap, and drain extension—can usually be maneuvered so that they will fit together. You may, however, have to buy and install some extra or replacement drain sections to complete a proper trap assembly. **NOTE:** On double-basin sinks, a common trap for both the disposer and the other basin is acceptable.

For a continuous-feed disposer, you will have to

install a switch. The most convenient place is on the bottom of the top rail of the sink cabinet, so when you open the cabinet door, the switch is at your fingertips. Or, you can mount the switch up in the backsplash area more than an arm's length from the disposer, so it cannot be turned on when a hand is in the disposer.

Check the disposer to see if any tools, screws or other materials have been dropped inside. Then, plug in the unit or install the switch and other wiring, following the manufacturer's directions and your local electrical code. Finally, test the disposer and check for leaks.

HOW TO INSTALL A DISHWASHER

Dishwashers have become as necessary as the sink, refrigerator, and range; in fact, there is hardly a new or remodeled kitchen to be found without one.

Dishwashers are available as built-ins or portable units. The latter include convertible models, sometimes called convertible/portables, that can be used first as portables and then later be installed under a counter. Because of consumer demand for built-in models, few true portables are made; most portables are the convertible type.

If you should decide a portable model would better suit your needs, expect to find units that can load from the front or the top. They will have power cords to plug in and hoses to attach to water faucets, and they will be on casters so you can roll them out of storage for use.

Convertibles look like portables, but their casters, hoses, and electrical cords can be removed when the unit is installed into a counter. On built-in dishwashers, such connections are made permanently when the unit is installed under the counter. Generally, convertible/portable models are slightly more expensive.

When you shop for a dishwasher, consider one that has an energy saver—a switch to eliminate the powered drying cycle. The dishes can air-dry instead, and you will save about 10 percent on energy.

Soft food disposers and screens that keep scraps from jamming a dishwasher pump are standard features on good dishwashers today. The number of cycles, however, varies widely, though most consumers' needs can be met by three—short wash, normal, and pots and pans. Select added cycles to suit your requirements. For example, a rinse-and-hold feature is handy if you have just a few dishes to wash on an infrequent basis. Santizing, plate-warming, and china-crystal are among other settings.

Dishes are dried by forced-air or convection (radiant) systems. The more common system is convection, which employs a heating element at the bottom of the tub. Forced-air drying uses a blower to force air over a heating element and then around the dishes.

Units have spray action on one, two, or three levels. Most quality dishwashers have two- or three-level spray action. The best results are achieved with spray arms at top and bottom, with a separate spray for the upper rack.

Other recommended features include porcelain enamel on steel interiors, detergent/rinse dispensers, removable silverware baskets, and adjustable upper racks.

For a decorative exterior, virtually every manufacturer uses a panel pack that allows a choice of four colors—two door inserts with a color on each side. Optional kits make it possible to have a black-glass door look or a door customized with paneling or other treatment to match a decorative theme.

Installing a new dishwasher is easier than putting in some other fixtures because you must hook up only the hot water supply line—cold water is not needed. To install a dishwasher, use the following general procedure:

If the dishwasher is to fit where you presently have a 24-inch cabinet, look for screws fastening the cabinet through the face frame to cabinets on either side. Remove them. Check for screws fastening the cabinet to the wall and take them out. There may also be screws through the corner gussets that fasten it to the countertop; these must also be removed.

The cabinet will be fitted tightly and you may have to take up the floor covering to slide it out. In pulling it out, be very careful not to chip or mar the cabinets on either side. In rare cases, you may find that the cabinet rests on a kick rail, rather than the kick rail being a part of the cabinet; the cabinet will come out more easily and will not disturb the floor covering, and you can simply saw out the piece of kick rail, flush at either side.

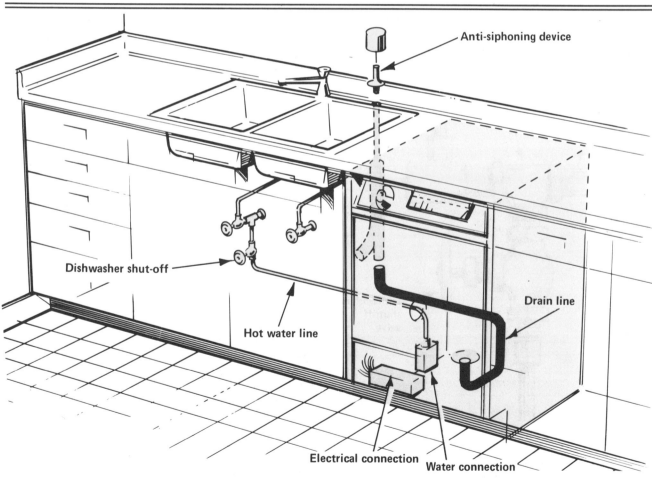

Anti-siphoning device

Dishwasher shut-off

Hot water line

Drain line

Electrical connection

Water connection

Exposed view of dishwasher showing water and electrical connections.

If, however, you are going to slide the dishwasher into place under a tiled countertop, do not remove any wood strips supporting the tile. Check the floor and wall first for any cracks that should be sealed to prevent insects from entering the house. Make sure you have a solid wood base under the countertop for fastening the dishwasher at the front. Usually there is ample room and screws will go directly through the tabs on the dishwasher into the countertop. If your countertop is Corian, holes will have to be drilled for the screws.

Now check your space and measure the dishwasher to make sure it will fit.

You will also need a separate 20-amp circuit for the dishwasher. It may be best to have a professional electrician put in this circuit.

The hot water supply line to your dishwasher should be ½-inch flexible copper tubing, and it should have a shutoff valve in a place where you can reach it.

Turn off the main water supply and hot water valve at your water heater. Open all house faucets and drain the pipes. Remove the hot water shutoff valve under the kitchen sink and install a T-fitting to the hot water supply stub-out. Reinstall the old shutoff valve that goes to the faucet, and install a new shutoff valve for the dishwasher line directly to the T-fitting. Now run flexible copper tubing from the T-fitting to the inlet valve on the dishwasher and connect it according to the manufacturer's instructions. Apply plumber's joint compound or tape to all threaded connections.

The drain line from the dishwasher can feed directly into your sink's food waste disposer—attaching to a plug designed for that purpose—or into the sink drainpipe. If you plan to connect the drain line into the sink drain, insert a waste T-fitting in the sink drainpipe between the tailpiece and the trap, or a new tailpiece with a T-fitting for this purpose. If the dishwasher drain hose has a threaded coupling, obtain a waste T-fitting with a threaded connection on its side; otherwise, the drain hose can be connected to a smooth side connection on the T-fitting by means of a hose clamp.

To connect the dishwasher's drain hose to a food waste disposer that has a short inlet pipe on its side, remove the knockout plug blocking the inlet pipe from inside the disposer. You can angle a screwdriver or punch against the plug and tap the tool with a hammer until the plug comes loose. Remove the plug from the disposer. Connect the drain hose from the dishwasher to the disposer's inlet pipe according to the manufacturer's instructions.

The dishwasher's drain hose must be routed up to above the highest level of water in the sink, to prevent siphoning. Hand-screw a hook into the bottom rear of the countertop, loop the hose over it, then drill a 1-inch hole in the side of the sink cabinet for the drain hose to enter. You might prefer to install an "air gap" anti-siphon device on the sink, routing the dishwasher drain up to it and then down to the disposer or drain. For this, you need an opening in the deck of the sink. However, this device can be mounted in the countertop. While plumbers recommended this device, kitchen installers usually find looping the drain will do the job. Behind the rear of the dishwasher, there will be room to run the loop up to the countertop and then down to the hole in the sink cabinet.

With all electrical and plumbing connections made, slide the dishwasher into place and screw it to the countertop through the two front tabs. Adjust the leveling legs at the base to make sure the unit is level.

Turn on the main water supply, and the hot water at the shutoff valve, and check all fittings for leaks. Run the dishwasher through a full cycle, again checking for leaks.

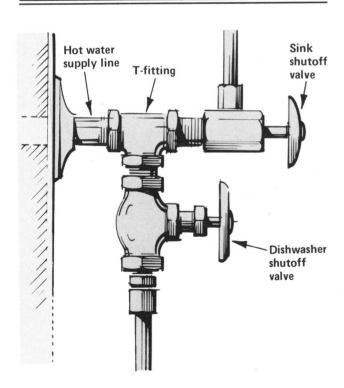

Hot water supply line

T-fitting

Sink shutoff valve

Dishwasher shutoff valve

The drawing shows how a T-fitting is used to provide a separate shutoff valve for a dishwasher at a sink's hot water supply line.